Lua 5.3
Reference Manual

The reference manual is the official definition of the Lua language.
For a complete introduction to Lua programming, see the book Programming in Lua.

Contents

Index

table.remove
table.sort
table.unpack

utf8
utf8.char
utf8.charpattern
utf8.codepoint
utf8.codes
utf8.len
utf8.offset

environment variables

LUA_CPATH
LUA_CPATH_5_3
LUA_INIT
LUA_INIT_5_3
LUA_PATH
LUA_PATH_5_3

C API

lua_Alloc
lua_CFunction
lua_Debug
lua_Hook
lua_Integer
lua_KContext
lua_KFunction
lua_Number
lua_Reader
lua_State
lua_Unsigned
lua_Writer

lua_absindex
lua_arith
lua_atpanic
lua_call
lua_callk
lua_checkstack
lua_close
lua_compare
lua_concat
lua_copy
lua_createtable
lua_dump
lua_error
lua_gc
lua_getallocf
lua_getextraspace
lua_getfield
lua_getglobal
lua_gethook
lua_gethookcount

lua_gethookmask
lua_geti
lua_getinfo
lua_getlocal
lua_getmetatable
lua_getstack
lua_gettable
lua_gettop
lua_getupvalue
lua_getuservalue
lua_insert
lua_isboolean
lua_iscfunction
lua_isfunction
lua_isinteger
lua_islightuserdata
lua_isnil
lua_isnone
lua_isnoneornil
lua_isnumber
lua_isstring
lua_istable
lua_isthread
lua_isuserdata
lua_isyieldable
lua_len
lua_load
lua_newstate
lua_newtable
lua_newthread
lua_newuserdata
lua_next
lua_numbertointeger
lua_pcall
lua_pcallk
lua_pop
lua_pushboolean
lua_pushcclosure
lua_pushcfunction
lua_pushfstring
lua_pushglobaltable
lua_pushinteger
lua_pushlightuserdata
lua_pushliteral
lua_pushlstring
lua_pushnil
lua_pushnumber
lua_pushstring
lua_pushthread
lua_pushvalue
lua_pushvfstring
lua_rawequal
lua_rawget
lua_rawgeti
lua_rawgetp
lua_rawlen
lua_rawset

lua_rawseti
lua_rawsetp
lua_register
lua_remove
lua_replace
lua_resume
lua_rotate
lua_setallocf
lua_setfield
lua_setglobal
lua_sethook
lua_seti
lua_setlocal
lua_setmetatable
lua_settable
lua_settop
lua_setupvalue
lua_setuservalue
lua_status
lua_stringtonumber
lua_toboolean
lua_tocfunction
lua_tointeger
lua_tointegerx
lua_tolstring
lua_tonumber
lua_tonumberx
lua_topointer
lua_tostring
lua_tothread
lua_touserdata
lua_type
lua_typename
lua_upvalueid
lua_upvalueindex
lua_upvaluejoin
lua_version
lua_xmove
lua_yield
lua_yieldk

auxiliary library

luaL_Buffer
luaL_Reg
luaL_Stream

luaL_addchar
luaL_addlstring
luaL_addsize
luaL_addstring
luaL_addvalue
luaL_argcheck
luaL_argerror
luaL_buffinit
luaL_buffinitsize
luaL_callmeta

luaL_checkany
luaL_checkinteger
luaL_checklstring
luaL_checknumber
luaL_checkoption
luaL_checkstack
luaL_checkstring
luaL_checktype
luaL_checkudata
luaL_checkversion
luaL_dofile
luaL_dostring
luaL_error
luaL_execresult
luaL_fileresult
luaL_getmetafield
luaL_getmetatable
luaL_getsubtable
luaL_gsub
luaL_len
luaL_loadbuffer
luaL_loadbufferx
luaL_loadfile
luaL_loadfilex
luaL_loadstring
luaL_newlib
luaL_newlibtable
luaL_newmetatable
luaL_newstate
luaL_openlibs
luaL_opt
luaL_optinteger
luaL_optlstring
luaL_optnumber
luaL_optstring
luaL_prepbuffer
luaL_prepbuffsize
luaL_pushresult
luaL_pushresultsize
luaL_ref
luaL_requiref

luaL_setfuncs
luaL_setmetatable
luaL_testudata
luaL_tolstring
luaL_traceback
luaL_typename
luaL_unref
luaL_where

standard library

luaopen_base
luaopen_coroutine
luaopen_debug
luaopen_io
luaopen_math
luaopen_os
luaopen_package
luaopen_string
luaopen_table
luaopen_utf8

constants

LUA_ERRERR
LUA_ERRFILE
LUA_ERRGCMM
LUA_ERRMEM
LUA_ERRRUN
LUA_ERRSYNTAX
LUA_HOOKCALL
LUA_HOOKCOUNT
LUA_HOOKLINE
LUA_HOOKRET
LUA_HOOKTAILCALL
LUA_MASKCALL
LUA_MASKCOUNT
LUA_MASKLINE
LUA_MASKRET
LUA_MAXINTEGER

LUA_MININTEGER
LUA_MINSTACK
LUA_MULTRET
LUA_NOREF
LUA_OK
LUA_OPADD
LUA_OPBAND
LUA_OPBNOT
LUA_OPBOR
LUA_OPBXOR
LUA_OPDIV
LUA_OPEQ
LUA_OPIDIV
LUA_OPLE
LUA_OPLT
LUA_OPMOD
LUA_OPMUL
LUA_OPPOW
LUA_OPSHL
LUA_OPSHR
LUA_OPSUB
LUA_OPUNM
LUA_REFNIL
LUA_REGISTRYINDEX
LUA_RIDX_GLOBALS
LUA_RIDX_MAINTHREAD
LUA_TBOOLEAN
LUA_TFUNCTION
LUA_TLIGHTUSERDATA
LUA_TNIL
LUA_TNONE
LUA_TNUMBER
LUA_TSTRING
LUA_TTABLE
LUA_TTHREAD
LUA_TUSERDATA
LUA_USE_APICHECK
LUA_YIELD
LUAL_BUFFERSIZE

1 – Introduction

Lua is a powerful, efficient, lightweight, embeddable scripting language. It supports procedural programming, object-oriented programming, functional programming, data-driven programming, and data description.

Lua combines simple procedural syntax with powerful data description constructs based on associative arrays and extensible semantics. Lua is dynamically typed, runs by interpreting bytecode with a register-based virtual machine, and has automatic memory management with incremental garbage collection, making it ideal for configuration, scripting, and rapid prototyping.

Lua is implemented as a library, written in *clean C*, the common subset of Standard C and C++. The Lua distribution includes a host program called `lua`, which uses the Lua library to offer a complete, standalone Lua interpreter, for interactive or batch use. Lua is intended to be used both as a powerful, lightweight, embeddable scripting language for any program that needs one, and as a powerful but lightweight and efficient stand-alone language.

As an extension language, Lua has no notion of a "main" program: it works *embedded* in a host client, called the *embedding program* or simply the *host*. (Frequently, this host is the stand-alone `lua` program.) The host program can invoke functions to execute a piece of Lua code, can write and read Lua variables, and can register C functions to be called by Lua code. Through the use of C functions, Lua can be augmented to cope with a wide range of different domains, thus creating customized programming languages sharing a syntactical framework.

Lua is free software, and is provided as usual with no guarantees, as stated in its license. The implementation described in this manual is available at Lua's official web site, `www.lua.org`.

Like any other reference manual, this document is dry in places. For a discussion of the decisions behind the design of Lua, see the technical papers available at Lua's web site. For a detailed introduction to programming in Lua, see Roberto's book, *Programming in Lua*.

2 – Basic Concepts

This section describes the basic concepts of the language.

2.1 – Values and Types

Lua is a *dynamically typed language*. This means that variables do not have types; only values do. There are no type definitions in the language. All values carry their own type.

All values in Lua are *first-class values*. This means that all values can be stored in variables, passed as arguments to other functions, and returned as results.

There are eight basic types in Lua: *nil*, *boolean*, *number*, *string*, *function*, *userdata*, *thread*, and *table*. The type *nil* has one single value, **nil**, whose main property is to be different from any other value; it usually represents the absence of a useful value. The type *boolean* has two values, **false** and **true**. Both **nil** and **false** make a condition false; any other value makes it true. The type *number* represents both integer numbers and real (floating-point) numbers. The type *string* represents immutable sequences of bytes. Lua is 8-bit clean: strings can contain any 8-bit value, including embedded zeros ('\0'). Lua is also encoding-agnostic; it makes no assumptions about the contents of a string.

The type *number* uses two internal representations, or two subtypes, one called *integer* and the other called *float*. Lua has explicit rules about when each representation is used, but it also converts between them automatically as needed (see §3.4.3). Therefore, the programmer may choose to mostly ignore the difference between integers and floats or to assume complete control over the representation of each number. Standard Lua uses 64-bit integers and double-precision (64-bit) floats, but you can also compile Lua so that it uses 32-bit integers and/or single-precision (32-bit) floats. The option with 32 bits for both integers and floats is particularly attractive for small machines and embedded systems. (See macro LUA_32BITS in file luaconf.h.)

Lua can call (and manipulate) functions written in Lua and functions written in C (see §3.4.10). Both are represented by the type *function*.

The type *userdata* is provided to allow arbitrary C data to be stored in Lua variables. A userdata value represents a block of raw memory. There are two kinds of userdata: *full userdata*, which is an object with a block of memory managed by Lua, and *light userdata*, which is simply a C pointer value. Userdata has no predefined operations in Lua, except assignment and identity test. By using *metatables*, the programmer can define operations for full userdata values (see §2.4). Userdata values cannot be created or modified in Lua, only through the C API. This guarantees the integrity of data owned by the host program.

The type *thread* represents independent threads of execution and it is used to implement coroutines (see §2.6). Lua threads are not related to operating-system threads. Lua supports coroutines on all systems, even those that do not support threads natively.

The type *table* implements associative arrays, that is, arrays that can be indexed not only with numbers, but with any Lua value except **nil** and NaN. (*Not a Number* is a special value used to represent undefined or unrepresentable numerical results, such as 0/0.) Tables can be *heterogeneous*; that is, they can contain values of all types (except **nil**). Any key with value **nil** is not considered part of the table. Conversely, any key that is not part of a table has an associated value **nil**.

Tables are the sole data-structuring mechanism in Lua; they can be used to represent ordinary arrays, sequences, symbol tables, sets, records, graphs, trees, etc. To represent records, Lua uses the field name as an index. The language supports this representation by providing a.name as syntactic sugar for a["name"]. There are several convenient ways to create tables in Lua (see §3.4.9).

We use the term *sequence* to denote a table where the set of all positive numeric keys is equal to {1..*n*} for some non-negative integer *n*, which is called the length of the sequence (see §3.4.7).

Like indices, the values of table fields can be of any type. In particular, because functions are first-class values, table fields can contain functions. Thus tables can also carry *methods* (see §3.4.11).

The indexing of tables follows the definition of raw equality in the language. The expressions a[i] and a[j] denote the same table element if and only if i and j are raw equal (that is, equal without metamethods). In particular, floats with integral values are equal to their respective integers (e.g., 1.0 == 1). To avoid ambiguities, any float with integral value used as a key is converted to its respective integer. For instance, if you write a[2.0] = true, the actual key inserted into the table will be the integer 2. (On the other hand, 2 and "2" are different Lua values and therefore denote different table entries.)

Tables, functions, threads, and (full) userdata values are *objects*: variables do not actually *contain* these values, only *references* to them. Assignment, parameter passing, and function returns always manipulate references to such values; these operations do not imply any kind of copy.

The library function type returns a string describing the type of a given value (see §6.1).

2.2 – Environments and the Global Environment

As will be discussed in §3.2 and §3.3.3, any reference to a free name (that is, a name not bound to any declaration) var is syntactically translated to _ENV.var. Moreover, every chunk is compiled in the scope of an external local variable named _ENV (see §3.3.2), so _ENV itself is never a free name in a chunk.

Despite the existence of this external _ENV variable and the translation of free names, _ENV is a completely regular name. In particular, you can define new variables and parameters with that name. Each reference to a free name uses the _ENV that is visible at that point in the program, following the usual visibility rules of Lua (see §3.5).

Any table used as the value of _ENV is called an *environment*.

Lua keeps a distinguished environment called the *global environment*. This value is kept at a special index in the C registry (see §4.5). In Lua, the global variable _G is initialized with this same value. (_G is never used internally.)

When Lua loads a chunk, the default value for its _ENV upvalue is the global environment (see load). Therefore, by default, free names in Lua code refer to entries in the global environment (and, therefore, they are also called *global variables*). Moreover, all standard libraries are loaded in the global environment and some functions there operate on that environment. You can use load (or loadfile) to load a chunk with a different environment. (In C, you have to load the chunk and then change the value of its first upvalue.)

2.3 – Error Handling

Because Lua is an embedded extension language, all Lua actions start from C code in the host program calling a function from the Lua library. (When you use Lua standalone, the lua application is the host program.) Whenever an error occurs during the compilation or execution of a Lua chunk, control returns to the host, which can take appropriate measures (such as printing an error message).

Lua code can explicitly generate an error by calling the error function. If you need to catch errors in Lua, you can use pcall or xpcall to call a given function in *protected mode*.

Whenever there is an error, an *error object* (also called an *error message*) is propagated with information about the error. Lua itself only generates errors whose error object is a string, but programs may generate errors with any value as the error object. It is up to the Lua program or its host to handle such error objects.

When you use `xpcall` or `lua_pcall`, you may give a *message handler* to be called in case of errors. This function is called with the original error object and returns a new error object. It is called before the error unwinds the stack, so that it can gather more information about the error, for instance by inspecting the stack and creating a stack traceback. This message handler is still protected by the protected call; so, an error inside the message handler will call the message handler again. If this loop goes on for too long, Lua breaks it and returns an appropriate message.

2.4 – Metatables and Metamethods

Every value in Lua can have a *metatable*. This *metatable* is an ordinary Lua table that defines the behavior of the original value under certain special operations. You can change several aspects of the behavior of operations over a value by setting specific fields in its metatable. For instance, when a non-numeric value is the operand of an addition, Lua checks for a function in the field "__add" of the value's metatable. If it finds one, Lua calls this function to perform the addition.

The key for each event in a metatable is a string with the event name prefixed by two underscores; the corresponding values are called *metamethods*. In the previous example, the key is "__add" and the metamethod is the function that performs the addition.

You can query the metatable of any value using the `getmetatable` function. Lua queries metamethods in metatables using a raw access (see `rawget`). So, to retrieve the metamethod for event ev in object o, Lua does the equivalent to the following code:

```
rawget(getmetatable(o) or {}, "__ev")
```

You can replace the metatable of tables using the `setmetatable` function. You cannot change the metatable of other types from Lua code (except by using the debug library (§6.10)); you should use the C API for that.

Tables and full userdata have individual metatables (although multiple tables and userdata can share their metatables). Values of all other types share one single metatable per type; that is, there is one single metatable for all numbers, one for all strings, etc. By default, a value has no metatable, but the string library sets a metatable for the string type (see §6.4).

A metatable controls how an object behaves in arithmetic operations, bitwise operations, order comparisons, concatenation, length operation, calls, and indexing. A metatable also can define a function to be called when a userdata or a table is garbage collected (§2.5).

For the unary operators (negation, length, and bitwise NOT), the metamethod is computed and called with a dummy second operand, equal to the first one. This extra operand is only to simplify Lua's internals (by making these operators behave like a binary operation) and may be removed in future versions. (For most uses this extra operand is irrelevant.)

A detailed list of events controlled by metatables is given next. Each operation is identified by its corresponding key.

> **__add:** the addition (+) operation. If any operand for an addition is not a number (nor a string coercible to a number), Lua will try to call a metamethod. First, Lua will check the first operand (even if it is valid). If that operand does not define a metamethod for __add, then Lua will check the second operand. If Lua can find a metamethod, it calls the metamethod with the two operands as arguments, and the result of the call (adjusted to one value) is the result of the operation. Otherwise, it raises an error.
> **__sub:** the subtraction (-) operation. Behavior similar to the addition operation.

__mul: the multiplication (*) operation. Behavior similar to the addition operation.

__div: the division (/) operation. Behavior similar to the addition operation.

__mod: the modulo (%) operation. Behavior similar to the addition operation.

__pow: the exponentiation (^) operation. Behavior similar to the addition operation.

__unm: the negation (unary -) operation. Behavior similar to the addition operation.

__idiv: the floor division (//) operation. Behavior similar to the addition operation.

__band: the bitwise AND (&) operation. Behavior similar to the addition operation, except that Lua will try a metamethod if any operand is neither an integer nor a value coercible to an integer (see §3.4.3).

__bor: the bitwise OR (|) operation. Behavior similar to the bitwise AND operation.

__bxor: the bitwise exclusive OR (binary ~) operation. Behavior similar to the bitwise AND operation.

__bnot: the bitwise NOT (unary ~) operation. Behavior similar to the bitwise AND operation.

__shl: the bitwise left shift (<<) operation. Behavior similar to the bitwise AND operation.

__shr: the bitwise right shift (>>) operation. Behavior similar to the bitwise AND operation.

__concat: the concatenation (..) operation. Behavior similar to the addition operation, except that Lua will try a metamethod if any operand is neither a string nor a number (which is always coercible to a string).

__len: the length (#) operation. If the object is not a string, Lua will try its metamethod. If there is a metamethod, Lua calls it with the object as argument, and the result of the call (always adjusted to one value) is the result of the operation. If there is no metamethod but the object is a table, then Lua uses the table length operation (see §3.4.7). Otherwise, Lua raises an error.

__eq: the equal (==) operation. Behavior similar to the addition operation, except that Lua will try a metamethod only when the values being compared are either both tables or both full userdata and they are not primitively equal. The result of the call is always converted to a boolean.

__lt: the less than (<) operation. Behavior similar to the addition operation, except that Lua will try a metamethod only when the values being compared are neither both numbers nor both strings. The result of the call is always converted to a boolean.

__le: the less equal (<=) operation. Unlike other operations, the less-equal operation can use two different events. First, Lua looks for the __le metamethod in both operands, like in the less than operation. If it cannot find such a metamethod, then it will try the __lt metamethod, assuming that a <= b is equivalent to not (b < a). As with the other comparison operators, the result is always a boolean. (This use of the __lt event can be removed in future versions; it is also slower than a real __le metamethod.)

__index: The indexing access table[key]. This event happens when table is not a table or when key is not present in table. The metamethod is looked up in table.

Despite the name, the metamethod for this event can be either a function or a table. If it is a function, it is called with table and key as arguments, and the result of the call (adjusted to one value) is the result of the operation. If it is a table, the final result is the result of indexing this table with key. (This indexing is regular, not raw, and therefore can trigger another metamethod.)

__newindex: The indexing assignment table[key] = value. Like the index event, this event happens when table is not a table or when key is not present in table. The metamethod is looked up in table.

Like with indexing, the metamethod for this event can be either a function or a table. If it is a function, it is called with table, key, and value as arguments. If it is a table, Lua does an indexing assignment to this table with the same key and value. (This assignment is regular, not raw, and therefore can trigger another metamethod.)

Whenever there is a __newindex metamethod, Lua does not perform the primitive assignment. (If necessary, the metamethod itself can call rawset to do the assignment.)

__call: The call operation `func(args)`. This event happens when Lua tries to call a non-function value (that is, `func` is not a function). The metamethod is looked up in `func`. If present, the metamethod is called with `func` as its first argument, followed by the arguments of the original call (`args`). All results of the call are the result of the operation. (This is the only metamethod that allows multiple results.)

It is a good practice to add all needed metamethods to a table before setting it as a metatable of some object. In particular, the __gc metamethod works only when this order is followed (see §2.5.1).

Because metatables are regular tables, they can contain arbitrary fields, not only the event names defined above. Some functions in the standard library (e.g., `tostring`) use other fields in metatables for their own purposes.

2.5 – Garbage Collection

Lua performs automatic memory management. This means that you do not have to worry about allocating memory for new objects or freeing it when the objects are no longer needed. Lua manages memory automatically by running a *garbage collector* to collect all *dead objects* (that is, objects that are no longer accessible from Lua). All memory used by Lua is subject to automatic management: strings, tables, userdata, functions, threads, internal structures, etc.

Lua implements an incremental mark-and-sweep collector. It uses two numbers to control its garbage-collection cycles: the *garbage-collector pause* and the *garbage-collector step multiplier*. Both use percentage points as units (e.g., a value of 100 means an internal value of 1).

The garbage-collector pause controls how long the collector waits before starting a new cycle. Larger values make the collector less aggressive. Values smaller than 100 mean the collector will not wait to start a new cycle. A value of 200 means that the collector waits for the total memory in use to double before starting a new cycle.

The garbage-collector step multiplier controls the relative speed of the collector relative to memory allocation. Larger values make the collector more aggressive but also increase the size of each incremental step. You should not use values smaller than 100, because they make the collector too slow and can result in the collector never finishing a cycle. The default is 200, which means that the collector runs at "twice" the speed of memory allocation.

If you set the step multiplier to a very large number (larger than 10% of the maximum number of bytes that the program may use), the collector behaves like a stop-the-world collector. If you then set the pause to 200, the collector behaves as in old Lua versions, doing a complete collection every time Lua doubles its memory usage.

You can change these numbers by calling `lua_gc` in C or `collectgarbage` in Lua. You can also use these functions to control the collector directly (e.g., stop and restart it).

2.5.1 – Garbage-Collection Metamethods

You can set garbage-collector metamethods for tables and, using the C API, for full userdata (see §2.4). These metamethods are also called *finalizers*. Finalizers allow you to coordinate Lua's garbage collection with external resource management (such as closing files, network or database connections, or freeing your own memory).

For an object (table or userdata) to be finalized when collected, you must *mark* it for finalization. You mark an object for finalization when you set its metatable and the metatable has a field indexed by the string "__gc". Note that if you set a metatable without a __gc field and later create that field in the metatable, the object will not be marked for finalization.

When a marked object becomes garbage, it is not collected immediately by the garbage collector. Instead, Lua puts it in a list. After the collection, Lua goes through that list. For each object in the list, it checks the object's __gc metamethod: If it is a function, Lua calls it with the object as its single argument; if the metamethod is not a function, Lua simply ignores it.

At the end of each garbage-collection cycle, the finalizers for objects are called in the reverse order that the objects were marked for finalization, among those collected in that cycle; that is, the first finalizer to be called is the one associated with the object marked last in the program. The execution of each finalizer may occur at any point during the execution of the regular code.

Because the object being collected must still be used by the finalizer, that object (and other objects accessible only through it) must be *resurrected* by Lua. Usually, this resurrection is transient, and the object memory is freed in the next garbage-collection cycle. However, if the finalizer stores the object in some global place (e.g., a global variable), then the resurrection is permanent. Moreover, if the finalizer marks a finalizing object for finalization again, its finalizer will be called again in the next cycle where the object is unreachable. In any case, the object memory is freed only in a GC cycle where the object is unreachable and not marked for finalization.

When you close a state (see lua_close), Lua calls the finalizers of all objects marked for finalization, following the reverse order that they were marked. If any finalizer marks objects for collection during that phase, these marks have no effect.

2.5.2 – Weak Tables

A *weak table* is a table whose elements are *weak references*. A weak reference is ignored by the garbage collector. In other words, if the only references to an object are weak references, then the garbage collector will collect that object.

A weak table can have weak keys, weak values, or both. A table with weak values allows the collection of its values, but prevents the collection of its keys. A table with both weak keys and weak values allows the collection of both keys and values. In any case, if either the key or the value is collected, the whole pair is removed from the table. The weakness of a table is controlled by the __mode field of its metatable. If the __mode field is a string containing the character 'k', the keys in the table are weak. If __mode contains 'v', the values in the table are weak.

A table with weak keys and strong values is also called an *ephemeron table*. In an ephemeron table, a value is considered reachable only if its key is reachable. In particular, if the only reference to a key comes through its value, the pair is removed.

Any change in the weakness of a table may take effect only at the next collect cycle. In particular, if you change the weakness to a stronger mode, Lua may still collect some items from that table before the change takes effect.

Only objects that have an explicit construction are removed from weak tables. Values, such as numbers and light C functions, are not subject to garbage collection, and therefore are not removed from weak tables (unless their associated values are collected). Although strings are subject to garbage collection, they do not have an explicit construction, and therefore are not removed from weak tables.

Resurrected objects (that is, objects being finalized and objects accessible only through objects being finalized) have a special behavior in weak tables. They are removed from weak values before running their finalizers, but are removed from weak keys only in the next collection after running their finalizers, when such objects are actually freed. This behavior allows the finalizer to access properties associated with the object through weak tables.

If a weak table is among the resurrected objects in a collection cycle, it may not be properly cleared until the next cycle.

2.6 – Coroutines

Lua supports coroutines, also called *collaborative multithreading*. A coroutine in Lua represents an independent thread of execution. Unlike threads in multithread systems, however, a coroutine only suspends its execution by explicitly calling a yield function.

You create a coroutine by calling `coroutine.create`. Its sole argument is a function that is the main function of the coroutine. The `create` function only creates a new coroutine and returns a handle to it (an object of type *thread*); it does not start the coroutine.

You execute a coroutine by calling `coroutine.resume`. When you first call `coroutine.resume`, passing as its first argument a thread returned by `coroutine.create`, the coroutine starts its execution by calling its main function. Extra arguments passed to `coroutine.resume` are passed as arguments to that function. After the coroutine starts running, it runs until it terminates or *yields*.

A coroutine can terminate its execution in two ways: normally, when its main function returns (explicitly or implicitly, after the last instruction); and abnormally, if there is an unprotected error. In case of normal termination, `coroutine.resume` returns **true**, plus any values returned by the coroutine main function. In case of errors, `coroutine.resume` returns **false** plus an error object.

A coroutine yields by calling `coroutine.yield`. When a coroutine yields, the corresponding `coroutine.resume` returns immediately, even if the yield happens inside nested function calls (that is, not in the main function, but in a function directly or indirectly called by the main function). In the case of a yield, `coroutine.resume` also returns **true**, plus any values passed to `coroutine.yield`. The next time you resume the same coroutine, it continues its execution from the point where it yielded, with the call to `coroutine.yield` returning any extra arguments passed to `coroutine.resume`.

Like `coroutine.create`, the `coroutine.wrap` function also creates a coroutine, but instead of returning the coroutine itself, it returns a function that, when called, resumes the coroutine. Any arguments passed to this function go as extra arguments to `coroutine.resume`. `coroutine.wrap` returns all the values returned by `coroutine.resume`, except the first one (the boolean error code). Unlike `coroutine.resume`, `coroutine.wrap` does not catch errors; any error is propagated to the caller.

As an example of how coroutines work, consider the following code:

```
function foo (a)
  print("foo", a)
  return coroutine.yield(2*a)
end

co = coroutine.create(function (a,b)
      print("co-body", a, b)
      local r = foo(a+1)
      print("co-body", r)
      local r, s = coroutine.yield(a+b, a-b)
      print("co-body", r, s)
      return b, "end"
end)

print("main", coroutine.resume(co, 1, 10))
print("main", coroutine.resume(co, "r"))
print("main", coroutine.resume(co, "x", "y"))
print("main", coroutine.resume(co, "x", "y"))
```

When you run it, it produces the following output:

```
co-body  1        10
foo      2
main     true     4
co-body  r
main     true     11        -9
co-body  x        y
main     true     10        end
main     false    cannot resume dead coroutine
```

You can also create and manipulate coroutines through the C API: see functions `lua_newthread`, `lua_resume`, and `lua_yield`.

3 – The Language

This section describes the lexis, the syntax, and the semantics of Lua. In other words, this section describes which tokens are valid, how they can be combined, and what their combinations mean.

Language constructs will be explained using the usual extended BNF notation, in which {*a*} means 0 or more *a*'s, and [*a*] means an optional *a*. Non-terminals are shown like non-terminal, keywords are shown like **kword**, and other terminal symbols are shown like '='. The complete syntax of Lua can be found in §9 at the end of this manual.

3.1 – Lexical Conventions

Lua is a free-form language. It ignores spaces (including new lines) and comments between lexical elements (tokens), except as delimiters between names and keywords.

Names (also called *identifiers*) in Lua can be any string of letters, digits, and underscores, not beginning with a digit and not being a reserved word. Identifiers are used to name variables, table fields, and labels.

The following *keywords* are reserved and cannot be used as names:

```
and       break     do        else      elseif    end
false     for       function  goto      if        in
local     nil       not       or        repeat    return
then      true      until     while
```

Lua is a case-sensitive language: and is a reserved word, but And and AND are two different, valid names. As a convention, programs should avoid creating names that start with an underscore followed by one or more uppercase letters (such as _VERSION).

The following strings denote other tokens:

```
+       -       *       /       %       ^       #
&       ~       |       <<      >>      //
==      ~=      <=      >=      <       >       =
(       )       {       }       [       ]       ::
;       :       ,       .       ..      ...
```

Literal strings can be delimited by matching single or double quotes, and can contain the following C-like escape sequences: '\a' (bell), '\b' (backspace), '\f' (form feed), '\n' (newline), '\r' (carriage return), '\t' (horizontal tab), '\v' (vertical tab), '\\' (backslash), '\"' (quotation mark [double quote]), and '\'' (apostrophe [single quote]). A backslash followed by a real newline results in a newline in the string. The escape sequence '\z' skips the following span of white-space characters, including line breaks; it is particularly useful to break and indent a long literal string into multiple lines without adding the newlines and spaces into the string contents.

Strings in Lua can contain any 8-bit value, including embedded zeros, which can be specified as '\0'. More generally, we can specify any byte in a literal string by its numeric value. This can be done with the escape sequence \x*XX*, where *XX* is a sequence of exactly two hexadecimal digits, or with the escape sequence *ddd*, where *ddd* is a sequence of up to three decimal digits. (Note that if a decimal escape sequence is to be followed by a digit, it must be expressed using exactly three digits.)

The UTF-8 encoding of a Unicode character can be inserted in a literal string with the escape sequence \u{*XXX*} (note the mandatory enclosing brackets), where *XXX* is a sequence of one or more hexadecimal digits representing the character code point.

Literal strings can also be defined using a long format enclosed by *long brackets*. We define an *opening long bracket of level n* as an opening square bracket followed by *n* equal signs followed by another opening square bracket. So, an opening long bracket of level 0 is written as `[[`, an opening long bracket of level 1 is written as `[=[`, and so on. A *closing long bracket* is defined similarly; for instance, a closing long bracket of level 4 is written as `]====]`. A *long literal* starts with an opening long bracket of any level and ends at the first closing long bracket of the same level. It can contain any text except a closing bracket of the same level. Literals in this bracketed form can run for several lines, do not interpret any escape sequences, and ignore long brackets of any other level. Any kind of end-of-line sequence (carriage return, newline, carriage return followed by newline, or newline followed by carriage return) is converted to a simple newline.

Any byte in a literal string not explicitly affected by the previous rules represents itself. However, Lua opens files for parsing in text mode, and the system file functions may have problems with some control characters. So, it is safer to represent non-text data as a quoted literal with explicit escape sequences for the non-text characters.

For convenience, when the opening long bracket is immediately followed by a newline, the newline is not included in the string. As an example, in a system using ASCII (in which 'a' is coded as 97, newline is coded as 10, and '1' is coded as 49), the five literal strings below denote the same string:

```
a = 'alo\n123"'
a = "alo\n123\""
a = '\97lo\10\04923"'
a = [[alo
123"]]
a = [==[
alo
123"]==]
```

A *numeric constant* (or *numeral*) can be written with an optional fractional part and an optional decimal exponent, marked by a letter 'e' or 'E'. Lua also accepts hexadecimal constants, which start with `0x` or `0X`. Hexadecimal constants also accept an optional fractional part plus an optional binary exponent, marked by a letter 'p' or 'P'. A numeric constant with a radix point or an exponent denotes a float; otherwise, if its value fits in an integer, it denotes an integer. Examples of valid integer constants are

```
3     345     0xff     0xBEBADA
```

Examples of valid float constants are

```
3.0     3.1416     314.16e-2     0.31416E1     34e1
0x0.1E  0xA23p-4   0X1.921FB54442D18P+1
```

A *comment* starts with a double hyphen (`--`) anywhere outside a string. If the text immediately after `--` is not an opening long bracket, the comment is a *short comment*, which runs until the end of the line. Otherwise, it is a *long comment*, which runs until the corresponding closing long bracket. Long comments are frequently used to disable code temporarily.

3.2 – Variables

Variables are places that store values. There are three kinds of variables in Lua: global variables, local variables, and table fields.

A single name can denote a global variable or a local variable (or a function's formal parameter, which is a particular kind of local variable):

```
        var ::= Name
```

Name denotes identifiers, as defined in §3.1.

Any variable name is assumed to be global unless explicitly declared as a local (see §3.3.7). Local variables are *lexically scoped*: local variables can be freely accessed by functions defined inside their scope (see §3.5).

Before the first assignment to a variable, its value is **nil**.

Square brackets are used to index a table:

```
        var ::= prefixexp '[' exp ']'
```

The meaning of accesses to table fields can be changed via metatables. An access to an indexed variable t[i] is equivalent to a call gettable_event(t,i). (See §2.4 for a complete description of the gettable_event function. This function is not defined or callable in Lua. We use it here only for explanatory purposes.)

The syntax var.Name is just syntactic sugar for var["Name"]:

```
        var ::= prefixexp '.' Name
```

An access to a global variable x is equivalent to _ENV.x. Due to the way that chunks are compiled, _ENV is never a global name (see §2.2).

3.3 – Statements

Lua supports an almost conventional set of statements, similar to those in Pascal or C. This set includes assignments, control structures, function calls, and variable declarations.

3.3.1 – Blocks

A block is a list of statements, which are executed sequentially:

```
        block ::= {stat}
```

Lua has *empty statements* that allow you to separate statements with semicolons, start a block with a semicolon or write two semicolons in sequence:

```
        stat ::= ';'
```

Function calls and assignments can start with an open parenthesis. This possibility leads to an ambiguity in Lua's grammar. Consider the following fragment:

```
    a = b + c
    (print or io.write)('done')
```

The grammar could see it in two ways:

```
    a = b + c(print or io.write)('done')

    a = b + c; (print or io.write)('done')
```

The current parser always sees such constructions in the first way, interpreting the open parenthesis as the start of the arguments to a call. To avoid this ambiguity, it is a good practice to always precede with a semicolon statements that start with a parenthesis:

```
    ;(print or io.write)('done')
```

A block can be explicitly delimited to produce a single statement:

```
stat ::= do block end
```

Explicit blocks are useful to control the scope of variable declarations. Explicit blocks are also sometimes used to add a **return** statement in the middle of another block (see §3.3.4).

3.3.2 – Chunks

The unit of compilation of Lua is called a *chunk*. Syntactically, a chunk is simply a block:

```
chunk ::= block
```

Lua handles a chunk as the body of an anonymous function with a variable number of arguments (see §3.4.11). As such, chunks can define local variables, receive arguments, and return values. Moreover, such anonymous function is compiled as in the scope of an external local variable called _ENV (see §2.2). The resulting function always has _ENV as its only upvalue, even if it does not use that variable.

A chunk can be stored in a file or in a string inside the host program. To execute a chunk, Lua first *loads* it, precompiling the chunk's code into instructions for a virtual machine, and then Lua executes the compiled code with an interpreter for the virtual machine.

Chunks can also be precompiled into binary form; see program `luac` and function `string.dump` for details. Programs in source and compiled forms are interchangeable; Lua automatically detects the file type and acts accordingly (see `load`).

3.3.3 – Assignment

Lua allows multiple assignments. Therefore, the syntax for assignment defines a list of variables on the left side and a list of expressions on the right side. The elements in both lists are separated by commas:

```
stat ::= varlist '=' explist
varlist ::= var {',' var}
explist ::= exp {',' exp}
```

Expressions are discussed in §3.4.

Before the assignment, the list of values is *adjusted* to the length of the list of variables. If there are more values than needed, the excess values are thrown away. If there are fewer values than needed, the list is extended with as many **nil**'s as needed. If the list of expressions ends with a function call, then all values returned by that call enter the list of values, before the adjustment (except when the call is enclosed in parentheses; see §3.4).

The assignment statement first evaluates all its expressions and only then the assignments are performed. Thus the code

```
i = 3
i, a[i] = i+1, 20
```

sets a[3] to 20, without affecting a[4] because the i in a[i] is evaluated (to 3) before it is assigned 4. Similarly, the line

```
x, y = y, x
```

exchanges the values of x and y, and

```
x, y, z = y, z, x
```

cyclically permutes the values of x, y, and z.

The meaning of assignments to global variables and table fields can be changed via metatables. An assignment to an indexed variable `t[i] = val` is equivalent to `settable_event(t,i,val)`. (See §2.4 for a complete description of the `settable_event` function. This function is not defined or callable in Lua. We use it here only for explanatory purposes.)

An assignment to a global name `x = val` is equivalent to the assignment `_ENV.x = val` (see §2.2).

3.3.4 – Control Structures

The control structures **if**, **while**, and **repeat** have the usual meaning and familiar syntax:

```
stat ::= while exp do block end
stat ::= repeat block until exp
stat ::= if exp then block {elseif exp then block} [else block] end
```

Lua also has a **for** statement, in two flavors (see §3.3.5).

The condition expression of a control structure can return any value. Both **false** and **nil** are considered false. All values different from **nil** and **false** are considered true (in particular, the number 0 and the empty string are also true).

In the **repeat–until** loop, the inner block does not end at the **until** keyword, but only after the condition. So, the condition can refer to local variables declared inside the loop block.

The **goto** statement transfers the program control to a label. For syntactical reasons, labels in Lua are considered statements too:

```
stat ::= goto Name
stat ::= label
label ::= '::' Name '::'
```

A label is visible in the entire block where it is defined, except inside nested blocks where a label with the same name is defined and inside nested functions. A goto may jump to any visible label as long as it does not enter into the scope of a local variable.

Labels and empty statements are called *void statements*, as they perform no actions.

The **break** statement terminates the execution of a **while**, **repeat**, or **for** loop, skipping to the next statement after the loop:

```
stat ::= break
```

A **break** ends the innermost enclosing loop.

The **return** statement is used to return values from a function or a chunk (which is an anonymous function). Functions can return more than one value, so the syntax for the **return** statement is

```
stat ::= return [explist] [';']
```

The **return** statement can only be written as the last statement of a block. If it is really necessary to **return** in the middle of a block, then an explicit inner block can be used, as in the idiom `do return end`, because now **return** is the last statement in its (inner) block.

3.3.5 – For Statement

The **for** statement has two forms: one numerical and one generic.

The numerical **for** loop repeats a block of code while a control variable runs through an arithmetic progression. It has the following syntax:

```
stat ::= for Name '=' exp ',' exp [',' exp] do block end
```

The *block* is repeated for *name* starting at the value of the first *exp*, until it passes the second *exp* by steps of the third *exp*. More precisely, a **for** statement like

```
for v = e1, e2, e3 do block end
```

is equivalent to the code:

```
do
  local var, limit, step = tonumber(e1), tonumber(e2), tonumber(e3)
  if not (var and limit and step) then error() end
  var = var - step
  while true do
    var = var + step
    if (step >= 0 and var > limit) or (step < 0 and var < limit) then
      break
    end
    local v = var
    block
  end
end
```

Note the following:

All three control expressions are evaluated only once, before the loop starts. They must all result in numbers.

var, *limit*, and *step* are invisible variables. The names shown here are for explanatory purposes only.

If the third expression (the step) is absent, then a step of 1 is used.

You can use **break** and **goto** to exit a **for** loop.

The loop variable v is local to the loop body. If you need its value after the loop, assign it to another variable before exiting the loop.

The generic **for** statement works over functions, called *iterators*. On each iteration, the iterator function is called to produce a new value, stopping when this new value is **nil**. The generic **for** loop has the following syntax:

```
stat ::= for namelist in explist do block end
namelist ::= Name {',' Name}
```

A **for** statement like

```
for var_1, ···, var_n in explist do block end
```

is equivalent to the code:

```
do
  local f, s, var = explist
  while true do
    local var_1, ···, var_n = f(s, var)
    if var_1 == nil then break end
    var = var_1
    block
  end
end
```

Note the following:

> *explist* is evaluated only once. Its results are an *iterator* function, a *state*, and an initial value for the first *iterator variable*.
> *f*, *s*, and *var* are invisible variables. The names are here for explanatory purposes only.
> You can use **break** to exit a **for** loop.
> The loop variables *var_i* are local to the loop; you cannot use their values after the **for** ends. If you need these values, then assign them to other variables before breaking or exiting the loop.

3.3.6 – Function Calls as Statements

To allow possible side-effects, function calls can be executed as statements:

```
stat ::= functioncall
```

In this case, all returned values are thrown away. Function calls are explained in §3.4.10.

3.3.7 – Local Declarations

Local variables can be declared anywhere inside a block. The declaration can include an initial assignment:

```
stat ::= local namelist ['=' explist]
```

If present, an initial assignment has the same semantics of a multiple assignment (see §3.3.3). Otherwise, all variables are initialized with **nil**.

A chunk is also a block (see §3.3.2), and so local variables can be declared in a chunk outside any explicit block.

The visibility rules for local variables are explained in §3.5.

3.4 – Expressions

The basic expressions in Lua are the following:

```
exp ::= prefixexp
exp ::= nil | false | true
exp ::= Numeral
exp ::= LiteralString
exp ::= functiondef
exp ::= tableconstructor
exp ::= '...'
exp ::= exp binop exp
exp ::= unop exp
prefixexp ::= var | functioncall | '(' exp ')'
```

Numerals and literal strings are explained in §3.1; variables are explained in §3.2; function definitions are explained in §3.4.11; function calls are explained in §3.4.10; table constructors are explained in §3.4.9. Vararg expressions, denoted by three dots ('...'), can only be used when directly inside a vararg function; they are explained in §3.4.11.

Binary operators comprise arithmetic operators (see §3.4.1), bitwise operators (see §3.4.2), relational operators (see §3.4.4), logical operators (see §3.4.5), and the concatenation operator (see §3.4.6). Unary operators comprise the unary minus (see §3.4.1), the unary bitwise NOT (see §3.4.2), the unary logical **not** (see §3.4.5), and the unary *length operator* (see §3.4.7).

Both function calls and vararg expressions can result in multiple values. If a function call is used as a statement (see §3.3.6), then its return list is adjusted to zero elements, thus discarding all returned values. If an expression is used as the last (or the only) element of a list of expressions, then no adjustment is made (unless the expression is enclosed in parentheses). In all other contexts, Lua adjusts the result list to one element, either discarding all values except the first one or adding a single **nil** if there are no values.

Here are some examples:

```
f()                -- adjusted to 0 results
g(f(), x)          -- f() is adjusted to 1 result
g(x, f())          -- g gets x plus all results from f()
a,b,c = f(), x     -- f() is adjusted to 1 result (c gets nil)
a,b = ...          -- a gets the first vararg parameter, b gets
                   -- the second (both a and b can get nil if there
                   -- is no corresponding vararg parameter)

a,b,c = x, f()     -- f() is adjusted to 2 results
a,b,c = f()        -- f() is adjusted to 3 results
return f()         -- returns all results from f()
return ...         -- returns all received vararg parameters
return x,y,f()     -- returns x, y, and all results from f()
{f()}              -- creates a list with all results from f()
{...}              -- creates a list with all vararg parameters
{f(), nil}         -- f() is adjusted to 1 result
```

Any expression enclosed in parentheses always results in only one value. Thus, (f(x,y,z)) is always a single value, even if f returns several values. (The value of (f(x,y,z)) is the first value returned by f or **nil** if f does not return any values.)

3.4.1 – Arithmetic Operators

Lua supports the following arithmetic operators:

+: addition
-: subtraction
*: multiplication
/: float division
//: floor division
%: modulo
^: exponentiation
-: unary minus

With the exception of exponentiation and float division, the arithmetic operators work as follows: If both operands are integers, the operation is performed over integers and the result is an integer. Otherwise, if both operands are numbers or strings that can be converted to numbers (see §3.4.3), then they are converted to floats, the operation is performed following the usual rules for floating-point arithmetic (usually the IEEE 754 standard), and the result is a float.

Exponentiation and float division (/) always convert their operands to floats and the result is always a float. Exponentiation uses the ISO C function pow, so that it works for non-integer exponents too.

Floor division (//) is a division that rounds the quotient towards minus infinity, that is, the floor of the division of its operands.

Modulo is defined as the remainder of a division that rounds the quotient towards minus infinity (floor division).

In case of overflows in integer arithmetic, all operations *wrap around*, according to the usual rules of two-complement arithmetic. (In other words, they return the unique representable integer that is equal modulo 2^{64} to the mathematical result.)

3.4.2 – Bitwise Operators

Lua supports the following bitwise operators:

> **&:** bitwise AND
> **|:** bitwise OR
> **~:** bitwise exclusive OR
> **>>:** right shift
> **<<:** left shift
> **~:** unary bitwise NOT

All bitwise operations convert its operands to integers (see §3.4.3), operate on all bits of those integers, and result in an integer.

Both right and left shifts fill the vacant bits with zeros. Negative displacements shift to the other direction; displacements with absolute values equal to or higher than the number of bits in an integer result in zero (as all bits are shifted out).

3.4.3 – Coercions and Conversions

Lua provides some automatic conversions between some types and representations at run time. Bitwise operators always convert float operands to integers. Exponentiation and float division always convert integer operands to floats. All other arithmetic operations applied to mixed numbers (integers and floats) convert the integer operand to a float; this is called the *usual rule*. The C API also converts both integers to floats and floats to integers, as needed. Moreover, string concatenation accepts numbers as arguments, besides strings.

Lua also converts strings to numbers, whenever a number is expected.

In a conversion from integer to float, if the integer value has an exact representation as a float, that is the result. Otherwise, the conversion gets the nearest higher or the nearest lower representable value. This kind of conversion never fails.

The conversion from float to integer checks whether the float has an exact representation as an integer (that is, the float has an integral value and it is in the range of integer representation). If it does, that representation is the result. Otherwise, the conversion fails.

The conversion from strings to numbers goes as follows: First, the string is converted to an integer or a float, following its syntax and the rules of the Lua lexer. (The string may have also leading and trailing spaces and a sign.) Then, the resulting number (float or integer) is converted to the type (float or integer) required by the context (e.g., the operation that forced the conversion).

All conversions from strings to numbers accept both a dot and the current locale mark as the radix character. (The Lua lexer, however, accepts only a dot.)

The conversion from numbers to strings uses a non-specified human-readable format. For complete control over how numbers are converted to strings, use the `format` function from the string library (see `string.format`).

3.4.4 – Relational Operators

Lua supports the following relational operators:

> **==:** equality

~=: inequality
<: less than
>: greater than
<=: less or equal
>=: greater or equal

These operators always result in **false** or **true**.

Equality (==) first compares the type of its operands. If the types are different, then the result is **false**. Otherwise, the values of the operands are compared. Strings are compared in the obvious way. Numbers are equal if they denote the same mathematical value.

Tables, userdata, and threads are compared by reference: two objects are considered equal only if they are the same object. Every time you create a new object (a table, userdata, or thread), this new object is different from any previously existing object. Closures with the same reference are always equal. Closures with any detectable difference (different behavior, different definition) are always different.

You can change the way that Lua compares tables and userdata by using the "eq" metamethod (see §2.4).

Equality comparisons do not convert strings to numbers or vice versa. Thus, "0"==0 evaluates to **false**, and t[0] and t["0"] denote different entries in a table.

The operator ~= is exactly the negation of equality (==).

The order operators work as follows. If both arguments are numbers, then they are compared according to their mathematical values (regardless of their subtypes). Otherwise, if both arguments are strings, then their values are compared according to the current locale. Otherwise, Lua tries to call the "lt" or the "le" metamethod (see §2.4). A comparison a > b is translated to b < a and a >= b is translated to b <= a.

Following the IEEE 754 standard, NaN is considered neither smaller than, nor equal to, nor greater than any value (including itself).

3.4.5 – Logical Operators

The logical operators in Lua are **and**, **or**, and **not**. Like the control structures (see §3.3.4), all logical operators consider both **false** and **nil** as false and anything else as true.

The negation operator **not** always returns **false** or **true**. The conjunction operator **and** returns its first argument if this value is **false** or **nil**; otherwise, **and** returns its second argument. The disjunction operator **or** returns its first argument if this value is different from **nil** and **false**; otherwise, **or** returns its second argument. Both **and** and **or** use short-circuit evaluation; that is, the second operand is evaluated only if necessary. Here are some examples:

```
10 or 20            --> 10
10 or error()       --> 10
nil or "a"          --> "a"
nil and 10          --> nil
false and error()   --> false
false and nil       --> false
false or nil        --> nil
10 and 20           --> 20
```

(In this manual, --> indicates the result of the preceding expression.)

3.4.6 – Concatenation

The string concatenation operator in Lua is denoted by two dots ('..'). If both operands are strings or numbers, then they are converted to strings according to the rules described in §3.4.3. Otherwise, the __concat metamethod is called (see §2.4).

3.4.7 – The Length Operator

The length operator is denoted by the unary prefix operator #. The length of a string is its number of bytes (that is, the usual meaning of string length when each character is one byte).

A program can modify the behavior of the length operator for any value but strings through the __len metamethod (see §2.4).

Unless a __len metamethod is given, the length of a table t is only defined if the table is a *sequence*, that is, the set of its positive numeric keys is equal to *{1..n}* for some non-negative integer *n*. In that case, *n* is its length. Note that a table like

```
{10, 20, nil, 40}
```

is not a sequence, because it has the key 4 but does not have the key 3. (So, there is no *n* such that the set *{1..n}* is equal to the set of positive numeric keys of that table.) Note, however, that non-numeric keys do not interfere with whether a table is a sequence.

3.4.8 – Precedence

Operator precedence in Lua follows the table below, from lower to higher priority:

```
or
and
<       >       <=      >=      ~=      ==
|
~
&
<<      >>
..
+       -
*       /       //      %
unary operators (not    #       -       ~)
^
```

As usual, you can use parentheses to change the precedences of an expression. The concatenation ('..') and exponentiation ('^') operators are right associative. All other binary operators are left associative.

3.4.9 – Table Constructors

Table constructors are expressions that create tables. Every time a constructor is evaluated, a new table is created. A constructor can be used to create an empty table or to create a table and initialize some of its fields. The general syntax for constructors is

```
tableconstructor ::= '{' [fieldlist] '}'
fieldlist ::= field {fieldsep field} [fieldsep]
field ::= '[' exp ']' '=' exp | Name '=' exp | exp
fieldsep ::= ',' | ';'
```

Each field of the form [exp1] = exp2 adds to the new table an entry with key exp1 and value exp2. A field of the form name = exp is equivalent to ["name"] = exp. Finally, fields of the form exp are equivalent to [i] = exp, where i are consecutive integers starting with 1. Fields in the other formats do not affect this counting. For example,

```
a = { [f(1)] = g; "x", "y"; x = 1, f(x), [30] = 23; 45 }
```

is equivalent to

```
do
  local t = {}
  t[f(1)] = g
  t[1] = "x"          -- 1st exp
  t[2] = "y"          -- 2nd exp
  t.x = 1             -- t["x"] = 1
  t[3] = f(x)         -- 3rd exp
  t[30] = 23
  t[4] = 45           -- 4th exp
  a = t
end
```

The order of the assignments in a constructor is undefined. (This order would be relevant only when there are repeated keys.)

If the last field in the list has the form exp and the expression is a function call or a vararg expression, then all values returned by this expression enter the list consecutively (see §3.4.10).

The field list can have an optional trailing separator, as a convenience for machine-generated code.

3.4.10 – Function Calls

A function call in Lua has the following syntax:

```
functioncall ::= prefixexp args
```

In a function call, first prefixexp and args are evaluated. If the value of prefixexp has type *function*, then this function is called with the given arguments. Otherwise, the prefixexp "call" metamethod is called, having as first parameter the value of prefixexp, followed by the original call arguments (see §2.4).

The form

```
functioncall ::= prefixexp ':' Name args
```

can be used to call "methods". A call v:name($args$) is syntactic sugar for v.name(v,$args$), except that v is evaluated only once.

Arguments have the following syntax:

```
args ::= '(' [explist] ')'
args ::= tableconstructor
args ::= LiteralString
```

All argument expressions are evaluated before the call. A call of the form f{$fields$} is syntactic sugar for f({$fields$}); that is, the argument list is a single new table. A call of the form f'$string$' (or f"$string$" or f[[$string$]]) is syntactic sugar for f('$string$'); that is, the argument list is a single literal string.

A call of the form return *functioncall* is called a *tail call*. Lua implements *proper tail calls* (or *proper tail recursion*): in a tail call, the called function reuses the stack entry of the calling function. Therefore, there is no limit on the number of nested tail calls that a program can execute. However, a tail call erases any debug information about the calling function. Note that a tail call only happens with a particular syntax, where the **return** has one single function call as argument; this syntax makes the calling function return exactly the returns of the called function. So, none of the following examples are tail calls:

```
return (f(x))        -- results adjusted to 1
return 2 * f(x)
return x, f(x)       -- additional results
f(x); return         -- results discarded
return x or f(x)     -- results adjusted to 1
```

3.4.11 – Function Definitions

The syntax for function definition is

```
functiondef ::= function funcbody
funcbody ::= '(' [parlist] ')' block end
```

The following syntactic sugar simplifies function definitions:

```
stat ::= function funcname funcbody
stat ::= local function Name funcbody
funcname ::= Name {'.' Name} [':' Name]
```

The statement

```
function f () body end
```

translates to

```
f = function () body end
```

The statement

```
function t.a.b.c.f () body end
```

translates to

```
t.a.b.c.f = function () body end
```

The statement

```
local function f () body end
```

translates to

```
local f; f = function () body end
```

not to

```
local f = function () body end
```

(This only makes a difference when the body of the function contains references to f.)

A function definition is an executable expression, whose value has type *function*. When Lua precompiles a chunk, all its function bodies are precompiled too. Then, whenever Lua executes the function definition, the function is *instantiated* (or *closed*). This function instance (or *closure*) is the final value of the expression.

Parameters act as local variables that are initialized with the argument values:

```
parlist ::= namelist [',' '...'] | '...'
```

When a function is called, the list of arguments is adjusted to the length of the list of parameters, unless the function is a *vararg function*, which is indicated by three dots ('...') at the end of its parameter list. A vararg function does not adjust its argument list; instead, it collects all extra arguments and supplies them to the function through a *vararg expression*, which is also written as three dots. The value of this expression is a list of all actual extra arguments, similar to a function with multiple results. If a vararg expression is used inside another expression or in the middle of a list of expressions, then its return list is adjusted to one element. If the expression is used as the last element of a list of expressions, then no adjustment is made (unless that last expression is enclosed in parentheses).

As an example, consider the following definitions:

```
function f(a, b) end
function g(a, b, ...) end
function r() return 1,2,3 end
```

Then, we have the following mapping from arguments to parameters and to the vararg expression:

```
CALL               PARAMETERS

f(3)               a=3, b=nil
f(3, 4)            a=3, b=4
f(3, 4, 5)         a=3, b=4
f(r(), 10)         a=1, b=10
f(r())             a=1, b=2

g(3)               a=3, b=nil, ... -->  (nothing)
g(3, 4)            a=3, b=4,   ... -->  (nothing)
g(3, 4, 5, 8)      a=3, b=4,   ... -->  5  8
g(5, r())          a=5, b=1,   ... -->  2  3
```

Results are returned using the **return** statement (see §3.3.4). If control reaches the end of a function without encountering a **return** statement, then the function returns with no results.

There is a system-dependent limit on the number of values that a function may return. This limit is guaranteed to be larger than 1000.

The *colon* syntax is used for defining *methods*, that is, functions that have an implicit extra parameter self. Thus, the statement

```
function t.a.b.c:f (params) body end
```

is syntactic sugar for

```
t.a.b.c.f = function (self, params) body end
```

3.5 – Visibility Rules

Lua is a lexically scoped language. The scope of a local variable begins at the first statement after its declaration and lasts until the last non-void statement of the innermost block that includes the declaration. Consider the following example:

```
x = 10                -- global variable
do                    -- new block
  local x = x         -- new 'x', with value 10
  print(x)            --> 10
  x = x+1
  do                  -- another block
```

```
      local x = x+1      -- another 'x'
      print(x)           --> 12
    end
    print(x)             --> 11
  end
  print(x)               --> 10   (the global one)
```

Notice that, in a declaration like local x = x, the new x being declared is not in scope yet, and so the second x refers to the outside variable.

Because of the lexical scoping rules, local variables can be freely accessed by functions defined inside their scope. A local variable used by an inner function is called an *upvalue*, or *external local variable*, inside the inner function.

Notice that each execution of a **local** statement defines new local variables. Consider the following example:

```
a = {}
local x = 20
for i=1,10 do
  local y = 0
  a[i] = function () y=y+1; return x+y end
end
```

The loop creates ten closures (that is, ten instances of the anonymous function). Each of these closures uses a different y variable, while all of them share the same x.

4 – The Application Program Interface

This section describes the C API for Lua, that is, the set of C functions available to the host program to communicate with Lua. All API functions and related types and constants are declared in the header file lua.h.

Even when we use the term "function", any facility in the API may be provided as a macro instead. Except where stated otherwise, all such macros use each of their arguments exactly once (except for the first argument, which is always a Lua state), and so do not generate any hidden side-effects.

As in most C libraries, the Lua API functions do not check their arguments for validity or consistency. However, you can change this behavior by compiling Lua with the macro LUA_USE_APICHECK defined.

4.1 – The Stack

Lua uses a *virtual stack* to pass values to and from C. Each element in this stack represents a Lua value (**nil**, number, string, etc.).

Whenever Lua calls C, the called function gets a new stack, which is independent of previous stacks and of stacks of C functions that are still active. This stack initially contains any arguments to the C function and it is where the C function pushes its results to be returned to the caller (see lua_CFunction).

For convenience, most query operations in the API do not follow a strict stack discipline. Instead, they can refer to any element in the stack by using an *index*: A positive index represents an absolute stack position (starting at 1); a negative index represents an offset relative to the top of the stack. More specifically, if the stack has *n* elements, then index 1 represents the first element (that is, the element that was pushed onto the stack first) and index *n* represents the last element; index -1 also represents the last element (that is, the element at the top) and index -*n* represents the first element.

4.2 – Stack Size

When you interact with the Lua API, you are responsible for ensuring consistency. In particular, *you are responsible for controlling stack overflow*. You can use the function lua_checkstack to ensure that the stack has enough space for pushing new elements.

Whenever Lua calls C, it ensures that the stack has space for at least LUA_MINSTACK extra slots. LUA_MINSTACK is defined as 20, so that usually you do not have to worry about stack space unless your code has loops pushing elements onto the stack.

When you call a Lua function without a fixed number of results (see lua_call), Lua ensures that the stack has enough space for all results, but it does not ensure any extra space. So, before pushing anything in the stack after such a call you should use lua_checkstack.

4.3 – Valid and Acceptable Indices

Any function in the API that receives stack indices works only with *valid indices* or *acceptable indices*.

A *valid index* is an index that refers to a position that stores a modifiable Lua value. It comprises stack indices between 1 and the stack top (1 ≤ abs(index) ≤ top) plus *pseudo-indices*, which represent some positions that are accessible to C code but that are not in the stack. Pseudo-indices are used to access the registry (see §4.5) and the upvalues of a C function (see §4.4).

Functions that do not need a specific mutable position, but only a value (e.g., query functions), can be called with acceptable indices. An *acceptable index* can be any valid index, but it also can be any positive index after the stack top within the space allocated for the stack, that is, indices up to the stack size. (Note that 0 is never an acceptable index.) Except when noted otherwise, functions in the API work with acceptable indices.

Acceptable indices serve to avoid extra tests against the stack top when querying the stack. For instance, a C function can query its third argument without the need to first check whether there is a third argument, that is, without the need to check whether 3 is a valid index.

For functions that can be called with acceptable indices, any non-valid index is treated as if it contains a value of a virtual type LUA_TNONE, which behaves like a nil value.

4.4 – C Closures

When a C function is created, it is possible to associate some values with it, thus creating a *C closure* (see lua_pushcclosure); these values are called *upvalues* and are accessible to the function whenever it is called.

Whenever a C function is called, its upvalues are located at specific pseudo-indices. These pseudo-indices are produced by the macro lua_upvalueindex. The first upvalue associated with a function is at index lua_upvalueindex(1), and so on. Any access to lua_upvalueindex(*n*), where *n* is greater than the number of upvalues of the current function (but not greater than 256, which is one plus the maximum number of upvalues in a closure), produces an acceptable but invalid index.

4.5 – Registry

Lua provides a *registry*, a predefined table that can be used by any C code to store whatever Lua values it needs to store. The registry table is always located at pseudo-index LUA_REGISTRYINDEX. Any C library can store data into this table, but it must take care to choose keys that are different from those used by other libraries, to avoid collisions. Typically, you should use as key a string containing your library name, or a light userdata with the address of a C object in your code, or any Lua object created by your code. As with variable names, string keys starting with an underscore followed by uppercase letters are reserved for Lua.

The integer keys in the registry are used by the reference mechanism (see luaL_ref) and by some predefined values. Therefore, integer keys must not be used for other purposes.

When you create a new Lua state, its registry comes with some predefined values. These predefined values are indexed with integer keys defined as constants in lua.h. The following constants are defined:

> **LUA_RIDX_MAINTHREAD:** At this index the registry has the main thread of the state. (The main thread is the one created together with the state.)
> **LUA_RIDX_GLOBALS:** At this index the registry has the global environment.

4.6 – Error Handling in C

Internally, Lua uses the C longjmp facility to handle errors. (Lua will use exceptions if you compile it as C++; search for LUAI_THROW in the source code for details.) When Lua faces any error (such as a memory allocation error, type errors, syntax errors, and runtime errors) it *raises* an error; that is, it does a long jump. A *protected environment* uses `setjmp` to set a recovery point; any error jumps to the most recent active recovery point.

If an error happens outside any protected environment, Lua calls a *panic function* (see `lua_atpanic`) and then calls `abort`, thus exiting the host application. Your panic function can avoid this exit by never returning (e.g., doing a long jump to your own recovery point outside Lua).

The panic function runs as if it were a message handler (see §2.3); in particular, the error object is at the top of the stack. However, there is no guarantee about stack space. To push anything on the stack, the panic function must first check the available space (see §4.2).

Most functions in the API can raise an error, for instance due to a memory allocation error. The documentation for each function indicates whether it can raise errors.

Inside a C function you can raise an error by calling `lua_error`.

4.7 – Handling Yields in C

Internally, Lua uses the C `longjmp` facility to yield a coroutine. Therefore, if a C function `foo` calls an API function and this API function yields (directly or indirectly by calling another function that yields), Lua cannot return to `foo` any more, because the `longjmp` removes its frame from the C stack.

To avoid this kind of problem, Lua raises an error whenever it tries to yield across an API call, except for three functions: `lua_yieldk`, `lua_callk`, and `lua_pcallk`. All those functions receive a *continuation function* (as a parameter named k) to continue execution after a yield.

We need to set some terminology to explain continuations. We have a C function called from Lua which we will call the *original function*. This original function then calls one of those three functions in the C API, which we will call the *callee function*, that then yields the current thread. (This can happen when the callee function is `lua_yieldk`, or when the callee function is either `lua_callk` or `lua_pcallk` and the function called by them yields.)

Suppose the running thread yields while executing the callee function. After the thread resumes, it eventually will finish running the callee function. However, the callee function cannot return to the original function, because its frame in the C stack was destroyed by the yield. Instead, Lua calls a *continuation function*, which was given as an argument to the callee function. As the name implies, the continuation function should continue the task of the original function.

As an illustration, consider the following function:

```
int original_function (lua_State *L) {
  ...      /* code 1 */
  status = lua_pcall(L, n, m, h);  /* calls Lua */
  ...      /* code 2 */
}
```

Now we want to allow the Lua code being run by `lua_pcall` to yield. First, we can rewrite our function like here:

```
int k (lua_State *L, int status, lua_KContext ctx) {
  ...  /* code 2 */
}

int original_function (lua_State *L) {
  ...      /* code 1 */
  return k(L, lua_pcall(L, n, m, h), ctx);
}
```

In the above code, the new function k is a *continuation function* (with type `lua_KFunction`), which should do all the work that the original function was doing after calling `lua_pcall`. Now, we must inform Lua that it must call k if the Lua code being executed by `lua_pcall` gets interrupted in some way (errors or yielding), so we rewrite the code as here, replacing `lua_pcall` by `lua_pcallk`:

```
int original_function (lua_State *L) {
  ...       /* code 1 */
  return k(L, lua_pcallk(L, n, m, h, ctx2, k), ctx1);
}
```

Note the external, explicit call to the continuation: Lua will call the continuation only if needed, that is, in case of errors or resuming after a yield. If the called function returns normally without ever yielding, `lua_pcallk` (and `lua_callk`) will also return normally. (Of course, instead of calling the continuation in that case, you can do the equivalent work directly inside the original function.)

Besides the Lua state, the continuation function has two other parameters: the final status of the call plus the context value (`ctx`) that was passed originally to `lua_pcallk`. (Lua does not use this context value; it only passes this value from the original function to the continuation function.) For `lua_pcallk`, the status is the same value that would be returned by `lua_pcallk`, except that it is `LUA_YIELD` when being executed after a yield (instead of `LUA_OK`). For `lua_yieldk` and `lua_callk`, the status is always `LUA_YIELD` when Lua calls the continuation. (For these two functions, Lua will not call the continuation in case of errors, because they do not handle errors.) Similarly, when using `lua_callk`, you should call the continuation function with `LUA_OK` as the status. (For `lua_yieldk`, there is not much point in calling directly the continuation function, because `lua_yieldk` usually does not return.)

Lua treats the continuation function as if it were the original function. The continuation function receives the same Lua stack from the original function, in the same state it would be if the callee function had returned. (For instance, after a `lua_callk` the function and its arguments are removed from the stack and replaced by the results from the call.) It also has the same upvalues. Whatever it returns is handled by Lua as if it were the return of the original function.

4.8 – Functions and Types

Here we list all functions and types from the C API in alphabetical order. Each function has an indicator like this: [-o, +p, x]

The first field, o, is how many elements the function pops from the stack. The second field, p, is how many elements the function pushes onto the stack. (Any function always pushes its results after popping its arguments.) A field in the form x|y means the function can push (or pop) x or y elements, depending on the situation; an interrogation mark '?' means that we cannot know how many elements the function pops/pushes by looking only at its arguments (e.g., they may depend on what is on the stack). The third field, x, tells whether the function may raise errors: '-' means the function never raises any error; 'm' means the function may raise out-of-memory errors and errors running a __gc metamethod; 'e' means the function may raise any errors (it can run arbitrary Lua code, either directly or through metamethods); 'v' means the function may raise an error on purpose.

lua_absindex

```
int lua_absindex (lua_State *L, int idx);
```
                                                                              [-0, +0, –]

Converts the acceptable index idx into an equivalent absolute index (that is, one that does not depend on the stack top).

lua_Alloc

```
typedef void * (*lua_Alloc) (void *ud,
                             void *ptr,
                             size_t osize,
                             size_t nsize);
```

The type of the memory-allocation function used by Lua states. The allocator function must provide a functionality similar to `realloc`, but not exactly the same. Its arguments are ud, an opaque pointer passed to `lua_newstate`; ptr, a pointer to the block being allocated/reallocated/freed; osize, the original size of the block or some code about what is being allocated; and nsize, the new size of the block.

When `ptr` is not NULL, osize is the size of the block pointed by `ptr`, that is, the size given when it was allocated or reallocated.

When `ptr` is NULL, osize encodes the kind of object that Lua is allocating. osize is any of LUA_TSTRING, LUA_TTABLE, LUA_TFUNCTION, LUA_TUSERDATA, or LUA_TTHREAD when (and only when) Lua is creating a new object of that type. When osize is some other value, Lua is allocating memory for something else.

Lua assumes the following behavior from the allocator function:

When nsize is zero, the allocator must behave like `free` and return NULL.

When nsize is not zero, the allocator must behave like `realloc`. The allocator returns NULL if and only if it cannot fulfill the request. Lua assumes that the allocator never fails when osize >= nsize.

Here is a simple implementation for the allocator function. It is used in the auxiliary library by `luaL_newstate`.

```
static void *l_alloc (void *ud, void *ptr, size_t osize,
                                            size_t nsize) {
  (void)ud;  (void)osize;  /* not used */
  if (nsize == 0) {
    free(ptr);
    return NULL;
  }
  else
    return realloc(ptr, nsize);
}
```

Note that Standard C ensures that `free(NULL)` has no effect and that `realloc(NULL,size)` is equivalent to `malloc(size)`. This code assumes that `realloc` does not fail when shrinking a block. (Although Standard C does not ensure this behavior, it seems to be a safe assumption.)

lua_arith

```
void lua_arith (lua_State *L, int op);
```
[-(2|1), +1, *e*]

Performs an arithmetic or bitwise operation over the two values (or one, in the case of negations) at the top of the stack, with the value at the top being the second operand, pops these values, and pushes the result of the operation. The function follows the semantics of the corresponding Lua operator (that is, it may call metamethods).

The value of op must be one of the following constants:

LUA_OPADD: performs addition (+)
LUA_OPSUB: performs subtraction (-)
LUA_OPMUL: performs multiplication (*)

LUA_OPDIV: performs float division (/)
LUA_OPIDIV: performs floor division (//)
LUA_OPMOD: performs modulo (%)
LUA_OPPOW: performs exponentiation (^)
LUA_OPUNM: performs mathematical negation (unary -)
LUA_OPBNOT: performs bitwise NOT (~)
LUA_OPBAND: performs bitwise AND (&)
LUA_OPBOR: performs bitwise OR (|)
LUA_OPBXOR: performs bitwise exclusive OR (~)
LUA_OPSHL: performs left shift (<<)
LUA_OPSHR: performs right shift (>>)

lua_atpanic

```
lua_CFunction lua_atpanic (lua_State *L, lua_CFunction panicf);                    [-0, +0, –]
```

Sets a new panic function and returns the old one (see §4.6).

lua_call

```
void lua_call (lua_State *L, int nargs, int nresults);               [-(nargs+1), +nresults, e]
```

Calls a function.

To call a function you must use the following protocol: first, the function to be called is pushed onto the stack; then, the arguments to the function are pushed in direct order; that is, the first argument is pushed first. Finally you call `lua_call`; nargs is the number of arguments that you pushed onto the stack. All arguments and the function value are popped from the stack when the function is called. The function results are pushed onto the stack when the function returns. The number of results is adjusted to nresults, unless nresults is LUA_MULTRET. In this case, all results from the function are pushed. Lua takes care that the returned values fit into the stack space, but it does not ensure any extra space in the stack. The function results are pushed onto the stack in direct order (the first result is pushed first), so that after the call the last result is on the top of the stack.

Any error inside the called function is propagated upwards (with a `longjmp`).

The following example shows how the host program can do the equivalent to this Lua code:

```
a = f("how", t.x, 14)
```

Here it is in C:

```
lua_getglobal(L, "f");                          /* function to be called */
lua_pushliteral(L, "how");                            /* 1st argument */
lua_getglobal(L, "t");                             /* table to be indexed */
lua_getfield(L, -1, "x");          /* push result of t.x (2nd arg) */
lua_remove(L, -2);                        /* remove 't' from the stack */
lua_pushinteger(L, 14);                              /* 3rd argument */
lua_call(L, 3, 1);        /* call 'f' with 3 arguments and 1 result */
lua_setglobal(L, "a");                              /* set global 'a' */
```

Note that the code above is *balanced*: at its end, the stack is back to its original configuration. This is considered good programming practice.

lua_callk

```
void lua_callk (lua_State *L,                          [-(nargs + 1), +nresults, e]
                int nargs,
```

```
                    int nresults,
                    lua_KContext ctx,
                    lua_KFunction k);
```

This function behaves exactly like `lua_call`, but allows the called function to yield (see §4.7).

lua_CFunction

```
typedef int (*lua_CFunction) (lua_State *L);
```

Type for C functions.

In order to communicate properly with Lua, a C function must use the following protocol, which defines the way parameters and results are passed: a C function receives its arguments from Lua in its stack in direct order (the first argument is pushed first). So, when the function starts, `lua_gettop(L)` returns the number of arguments received by the function. The first argument (if any) is at index 1 and its last argument is at index `lua_gettop(L)`. To return values to Lua, a C function just pushes them onto the stack, in direct order (the first result is pushed first), and returns the number of results. Any other value in the stack below the results will be properly discarded by Lua. Like a Lua function, a C function called by Lua can also return many results.

As an example, the following function receives a variable number of numeric arguments and returns their average and their sum:

```
static int foo (lua_State *L) {
  int n = lua_gettop(L);    /* number of arguments */
  lua_Number sum = 0.0;
  int i;
  for (i = 1; i <= n; i++) {
    if (!lua_isnumber(L, i)) {
      lua_pushliteral(L, "incorrect argument");
      lua_error(L);
    }
    sum += lua_tonumber(L, i);
  }
  lua_pushnumber(L, sum/n);        /* first result */
  lua_pushnumber(L, sum);          /* second result */
  return 2;                    /* number of results */
}
```

lua_checkstack

```
int lua_checkstack (lua_State *L, int n);
```
[-0, +0, –]

Ensures that the stack has space for at least n extra slots (that is, that you can safely push up to n values into it). It returns false if it cannot fulfill the request, either because it would cause the stack to be larger than a fixed maximum size (typically at least several thousand elements) or because it cannot allocate memory for the extra space. This function never shrinks the stack; if the stack already has space for the extra slots, it is left unchanged.

lua_close

```
void lua_close (lua_State *L);
```
[-0, +0, –]

Destroys all objects in the given Lua state (calling the corresponding garbage-collection metamethods, if any) and frees all dynamic memory used by this state. On several platforms, you may not need to call this function, because all resources are naturally released when the host program ends. On the other hand, long-running programs that create multiple states, such as daemons or web servers, will probably need to close states as soon as they are not needed.

lua_compare

```
int lua_compare (lua_State *L, int index1, int index2, int op);                [-0, +0, e]
```

Compares two Lua values. Returns 1 if the value at index index1 satisfies op when compared with the value at index index2, following the semantics of the corresponding Lua operator (that is, it may call metamethods). Otherwise returns 0. Also returns 0 if any of the indices is not valid.

The value of op must be one of the following constants:

LUA_OPEQ: compares for equality (==)
LUA_OPLT: compares for less than (<)
LUA_OPLE: compares for less or equal (<=)

lua_concat

```
void lua_concat (lua_State *L, int n);                                          [-n, +1, e]
```

Concatenates the n values at the top of the stack, pops them, and leaves the result at the top. If n is 1, the result is the single value on the stack (that is, the function does nothing); if n is 0, the result is the empty string. Concatenation is performed following the usual semantics of Lua (see §3.4.6).

lua_copy

```
void lua_copy (lua_State *L, int fromidx, int toidx);                           [-0, +0, –]
```

Copies the element at index fromidx into the valid index toidx, replacing the value at that position. Values at other positions are not affected.

lua_createtable

```
void lua_createtable (lua_State *L, int narr, int nrec);                        [-0, +1, m]
```

Creates a new empty table and pushes it onto the stack. Parameter narr is a hint for how many elements the table will have as a sequence; parameter nrec is a hint for how many other elements the table will have. Lua may use these hints to preallocate memory for the new table. This preallocation is useful for performance when you know in advance how many elements the table will have. Otherwise you can use the function lua_newtable.

lua_dump

```
int lua_dump (lua_State *L,                                                     [-0, +0, –]
              lua_Writer writer,
              void *data,
              int strip);
```

Dumps a function as a binary chunk. Receives a Lua function on the top of the stack and produces a binary chunk that, if loaded again, results in a function equivalent to the one dumped. As it produces parts of the chunk, lua_dump calls function writer (see lua_Writer) with the given data to write them.

If strip is true, the binary representation may not include all debug information about the function, to save space.

The value returned is the error code returned by the last call to the writer; 0 means no errors.

This function does not pop the Lua function from the stack.

lua_error

```
int lua_error (lua_State *L);
```
[-1, +0, v]

Generates a Lua error, using the value at the top of the stack as the error object. This function does a long jump, and therefore never returns (see `luaL_error`).

lua_gc

```
int lua_gc (lua_State *L, int what, int data);
```
[-0, +0, m]

Controls the garbage collector.

This function performs several tasks, according to the value of the parameter `what`:

> **LUA_GCSTOP:** stops the garbage collector.
> **LUA_GCRESTART:** restarts the garbage collector.
> **LUA_GCCOLLECT:** performs a full garbage-collection cycle.
> **LUA_GCCOUNT:** returns the current amount of memory (in Kbytes) in use by Lua.
> **LUA_GCCOUNTB:** returns the remainder of dividing the current amount of bytes of memory in use by Lua by 1024.
> **LUA_GCSTEP:** performs an incremental step of garbage collection.
> **LUA_GCSETPAUSE:** sets `data` as the new value for the *pause* of the collector (see §2.5) and returns the previous value of the pause.
> **LUA_GCSETSTEPMUL:** sets `data` as the new value for the *step multiplier* of the collector (see §2.5) and returns the previous value of the step multiplier.
> **LUA_GCISRUNNING:** returns a boolean that tells whether the collector is running (i.e., not stopped).

For more details about these options, see `collectgarbage`.

lua_getallocf

```
lua_Alloc lua_getallocf (lua_State *L, void **ud);
```
[-0, +0, –]

Returns the memory-allocation function of a given state. If ud is not NULL, Lua stores in *ud the opaque pointer given when the memory-allocator function was set.

lua_getfield

```
int lua_getfield (lua_State *L, int index, const char *k);
```
[-0, +1, e]

Pushes onto the stack the value t[k], where t is the value at the given index. As in Lua, this function may trigger a metamethod for the "index" event (see §2.4).

Returns the type of the pushed value.

lua_getextraspace

```
void *lua_getextraspace (lua_State *L);
```
[-0, +0, –]

Returns a pointer to a raw memory area associated with the given Lua state. The application can use this area for any purpose; Lua does not use it for anything.

Each new thread has this area initialized with a copy of the area of the main thread.

By default, this area has the size of a pointer to void, but you can recompile Lua with a different size for this area. (See LUA_EXTRASPACE in luaconf.h.)

lua_getglobal

```
int lua_getglobal (lua_State *L, const char *name);                    [-0, +1, e]
```

Pushes onto the stack the value of the global name. Returns the type of that value.

lua_geti

```
int lua_geti (lua_State *L, int index, lua_Integer i);                 [-0, +1, e]
```

Pushes onto the stack the value t[i], where t is the value at the given index. As in Lua, this function may trigger a metamethod for the "index" event (see §2.4).

Returns the type of the pushed value.

lua_getmetatable

```
int lua_getmetatable (lua_State *L, int index);                        [-0, +(0|1), –]
```

If the value at the given index has a metatable, the function pushes that metatable onto the stack and returns 1. Otherwise, the function returns 0 and pushes nothing on the stack.

lua_gettable

```
int lua_gettable (lua_State *L, int index);                            [-1, +1, e]
```

Pushes onto the stack the value t[k], where t is the value at the given index and k is the value at the top of the stack.

This function pops the key from the stack, pushing the resulting value in its place. As in Lua, this function may trigger a metamethod for the "index" event (see §2.4).

Returns the type of the pushed value.

lua_gettop

```
int lua_gettop (lua_State *L);                                         [-0, +0, –]
```

Returns the index of the top element in the stack. Because indices start at 1, this result is equal to the number of elements in the stack; in particular, 0 means an empty stack.

lua_getuservalue

```
int lua_getuservalue (lua_State *L, int index);                        [-0, +1, –]
```

Pushes onto the stack the Lua value associated with the userdata at the given index.

Returns the type of the pushed value.

lua_insert

```
void lua_insert (lua_State *L, int index);                             [-1, +1, –]
```

Moves the top element into the given valid index, shifting up the elements above this index to open space. This function cannot be called with a pseudo-index, because a pseudo-index is not an actual stack position.

lua_Integer

```
typedef ... lua_Integer;
```

The type of integers in Lua.

By default this type is `long long`, (usually a 64-bit two-complement integer), but that can be changed to `long` or `int` (usually a 32-bit two-complement integer). (See `LUA_INT_TYPE` in `luaconf.h`.)

Lua also defines the constants `LUA_MININTEGER` and `LUA_MAXINTEGER`, with the minimum and the maximum values that fit in this type.

lua_isboolean

```
int lua_isboolean (lua_State *L, int index);                          [-0, +0, –]
```

Returns 1 if the value at the given index is a boolean, and 0 otherwise.

lua_iscfunction

```
int lua_iscfunction (lua_State *L, int index);                        [-0, +0, –]
```

Returns 1 if the value at the given index is a C function, and 0 otherwise.

lua_isfunction

```
int lua_isfunction (lua_State *L, int index);                         [-0, +0, –]
```

Returns 1 if the value at the given index is a function (either C or Lua), and 0 otherwise.

lua_isinteger

```
int lua_isinteger (lua_State *L, int index);                          [-0, +0, –]
```

Returns 1 if the value at the given index is an integer (that is, the value is a number and is represented as an integer), and 0 otherwise.

lua_islightuserdata

```
int lua_islightuserdata (lua_State *L, int index);                    [-0, +0, –]
```

Returns 1 if the value at the given index is a light userdata, and 0 otherwise.

lua_isnil

```
int lua_isnil (lua_State *L, int index);                              [-0, +0, –]
```

Returns 1 if the value at the given index is **nil**, and 0 otherwise.

lua_isnone

```
int lua_isnone (lua_State *L, int index);                             [-0, +0, –]
```

Returns 1 if the given index is not valid, and 0 otherwise.

lua_isnoneornil

[-0, +0, –]

```
int lua_isnoneornil (lua_State *L, int index);
```

Returns 1 if the given index is not valid or if the value at this index is **nil**, and 0 otherwise.

lua_isnumber

```
int lua_isnumber (lua_State *L, int index);
```
[-0, +0, –]

Returns 1 if the value at the given index is a number or a string convertible to a number, and 0 otherwise.

lua_isstring

```
int lua_isstring (lua_State *L, int index);
```
[-0, +0, –]

Returns 1 if the value at the given index is a string or a number (which is always convertible to a string), and 0 otherwise.

lua_istable

```
int lua_istable (lua_State *L, int index);
```
[-0, +0, –]

Returns 1 if the value at the given index is a table, and 0 otherwise.

lua_isthread

```
int lua_isthread (lua_State *L, int index);
```
[-0, +0, –]

Returns 1 if the value at the given index is a thread, and 0 otherwise.

lua_isuserdata

```
int lua_isuserdata (lua_State *L, int index);
```
[-0, +0, –]

Returns 1 if the value at the given index is a userdata (either full or light), and 0 otherwise.

lua_isyieldable

```
int lua_isyieldable (lua_State *L);
```
[-0, +0, –]

Returns 1 if the given coroutine can yield, and 0 otherwise.

lua_KContext

```
typedef ... lua_KContext;
```

The type for continuation-function contexts. It must be a numeric type. This type is defined as `intptr_t` when `intptr_t` is available, so that it can store pointers too. Otherwise, it is defined as `ptrdiff_t`.

lua_KFunction

```
typedef int (*lua_KFunction) (lua_State *L, int status, lua_KContext ctx);
```

Type for continuation functions (see §4.7).

lua_len

```
void lua_len (lua_State *L, int index);                               [-0, +1, e]
```

Returns the length of the value at the given index. It is equivalent to the '#' operator in Lua (see §3.4.7) and may trigger a metamethod for the "length" event (see §2.4). The result is pushed on the stack.

lua_load

```
int lua_load (lua_State *L,                                           [-0, +1, -]
              lua_Reader reader,
              void *data,
              const char *chunkname,
              const char *mode);
```

Loads a Lua chunk without running it. If there are no errors, lua_load pushes the compiled chunk as a Lua function on top of the stack. Otherwise, it pushes an error message.

The return values of lua_load are:

> **LUA_OK:** no errors;
> **LUA_ERRSYNTAX:** syntax error during precompilation;
> **LUA_ERRMEM:** memory allocation (out-of-memory) error;
> **LUA_ERRGCMM:** error while running a __gc metamethod. (This error has no relation with the chunk being loaded. It is generated by the garbage collector.)

The lua_load function uses a user-supplied reader function to read the chunk (see lua_Reader). The data argument is an opaque value passed to the reader function.

The chunkname argument gives a name to the chunk, which is used for error messages and in debug information (see §4.9).

lua_load automatically detects whether the chunk is text or binary and loads it accordingly (see program luac). The string mode works as in function load, with the addition that a NULL value is equivalent to the string "bt".

lua_load uses the stack internally, so the reader function must always leave the stack unmodified when returning.

If the resulting function has upvalues, its first upvalue is set to the value of the global environment stored at index LUA_RIDX_GLOBALS in the registry (see §4.5). When loading main chunks, this upvalue will be the _ENV variable (see §2.2). Other upvalues are initialized with **nil**.

lua_newstate

```
lua_State *lua_newstate (lua_Alloc f, void *ud);                      [-0, +0, -]
```

Creates a new thread running in a new, independent state. Returns NULL if it cannot create the thread or the state (due to lack of memory). The argument f is the allocator function; Lua does all memory allocation for this state through this function. The second argument, ud, is an opaque pointer that Lua passes to the allocator in every call.

lua_newtable

```
void lua_newtable (lua_State *L);                                     [-0, +1, m]
```

Creates a new empty table and pushes it onto the stack. It is equivalent to lua_createtable(L, 0, 0).

lua_newthread

```
lua_State *lua_newthread (lua_State *L);
```
[-0, +1, *m*]

Creates a new thread, pushes it on the stack, and returns a pointer to a `lua_State` that represents this new thread. The new thread returned by this function shares with the original thread its global environment, but has an independent execution stack.

There is no explicit function to close or to destroy a thread. Threads are subject to garbage collection, like any Lua object.

lua_newuserdata

```
void *lua_newuserdata (lua_State *L, size_t size);
```
[-0, +1, *m*]

This function allocates a new block of memory with the given size, pushes onto the stack a new full userdata with the block address, and returns this address. The host program can freely use this memory.

lua_next

```
int lua_next (lua_State *L, int index);
```
[-1, +(2|0), *e*]

Pops a key from the stack, and pushes a key–value pair from the table at the given index (the "next" pair after the given key). If there are no more elements in the table, then `lua_next` returns 0 (and pushes nothing).

A typical traversal looks like this:

```
/* table is in the stack at index 't' */
lua_pushnil(L);  /* first key */
while (lua_next(L, t) != 0) {
  /* uses 'key' (at index -2) and 'value' (at index -1) */
  printf("%s - %s\n",
          lua_typename(L, lua_type(L, -2)),
          lua_typename(L, lua_type(L, -1)));
  /* removes 'value'; keeps 'key' for next iteration */
  lua_pop(L, 1);
}
```

While traversing a table, do not call `lua_tolstring` directly on a key, unless you know that the key is actually a string. Recall that `lua_tolstring` may change the value at the given index; this confuses the next call to `lua_next`.

See function `next` for the caveats of modifying the table during its traversal.

lua_Number

```
typedef ... lua_Number;
```

The type of floats in Lua.

By default this type is double, but that can be changed to a single float or a long double. (See `LUA_FLOAT_TYPE` in `luaconf.h`.)

lua_numbertointeger

```
int lua_numbertointeger (lua_Number n, lua_Integer *p);
```

Converts a Lua float to a Lua integer. This macro assumes that n has an integral value. If that value is within the range of Lua integers, it is converted to an integer and assigned to *p. The macro results in a boolean indicating whether the conversion was successful. (Note that this range test can be tricky to do correctly without this macro, due to roundings.)

This macro may evaluate its arguments more than once.

lua_pcall

```
int lua_pcall (lua_State *L, int nargs, int nresults, int msgh);
```
[-(nargs + 1), +(nresults|1), –]

Calls a function in protected mode.

Both `nargs` and `nresults` have the same meaning as in `lua_call`. If there are no errors during the call, `lua_pcall` behaves exactly like `lua_call`. However, if there is any error, `lua_pcall` catches it, pushes a single value on the stack (the error object), and returns an error code. Like `lua_call`, `lua_pcall` always removes the function and its arguments from the stack.

If `msgh` is 0, then the error object returned on the stack is exactly the original error object. Otherwise, `msgh` is the stack index of a *message handler*. (This index cannot be a pseudo-index.) In case of runtime errors, this function will be called with the error object and its return value will be the object returned on the stack by `lua_pcall`.

Typically, the message handler is used to add more debug information to the error object, such as a stack traceback. Such information cannot be gathered after the return of `lua_pcall`, since by then the stack has unwound.

The `lua_pcall` function returns one of the following constants (defined in `lua.h`):

> **LUA_OK (0):** success.
> **LUA_ERRRUN:** a runtime error.
> **LUA_ERRMEM:** memory allocation error. For such errors, Lua does not call the message handler.
> **LUA_ERRERR:** error while running the message handler.
> **LUA_ERRGCMM:** error while running a __gc metamethod. (This error typically has no relation with the function being called.)

lua_pcallk

```
int lua_pcallk (lua_State *L,
                int nargs,
                int nresults,
                int msgh,
                lua_KContext ctx,
                lua_KFunction k);
```
[-(nargs + 1), +(nresults|1), –]

This function behaves exactly like `lua_pcall`, but allows the called function to yield (see §4.7).

lua_pop

```
void lua_pop (lua_State *L, int n);
```
[-n, +0, –]

Pops n elements from the stack.

lua_pushboolean

```
void lua_pushboolean (lua_State *L, int b);
```
[-0, +1, –]

Pushes a boolean value with value b onto the stack.

lua_pushcclosure

```
void lua_pushcclosure (lua_State *L, lua_CFunction fn, int n);
```
[-n, +1, *m*]

Pushes a new C closure onto the stack.

When a C function is created, it is possible to associate some values with it, thus creating a C closure (see §4.4); these values are then accessible to the function whenever it is called. To associate values with a C function, first these values must be pushed onto the stack (when there are multiple values, the first value is pushed first). Then `lua_pushcclosure` is called to create and push the C function onto the stack, with the argument n telling how many values will be associated with the function. `lua_pushcclosure` also pops these values from the stack.

The maximum value for n is 255.

When n is zero, this function creates a *light C function*, which is just a pointer to the C function. In that case, it never raises a memory error.

lua_pushcfunction

```
void lua_pushcfunction (lua_State *L, lua_CFunction f);
```
[-0, +1, –]

Pushes a C function onto the stack. This function receives a pointer to a C function and pushes onto the stack a Lua value of type `function` that, when called, invokes the corresponding C function.

Any function to be callable by Lua must follow the correct protocol to receive its parameters and return its results (see `lua_CFunction`).

lua_pushfstring

```
const char *lua_pushfstring (lua_State *L, const char *fmt, ...);
```
[-0, +1, e]

Pushes onto the stack a formatted string and returns a pointer to this string. It is similar to the ISO C function `sprintf`, but has some important differences:

> You do not have to allocate space for the result: the result is a Lua string and Lua takes care of memory allocation (and deallocation, through garbage collection).
> The conversion specifiers are quite restricted. There are no flags, widths, or precisions. The conversion specifiers can only be '%%' (inserts the character '%'), '%s' (inserts a zero-terminated string, with no size restrictions), '%f' (inserts a `lua_Number`), '%I' (inserts a `lua_Integer`), '%p' (inserts a pointer as a hexadecimal numeral), '%d' (inserts an int), '%c' (inserts an int as a one-byte character), and '%U' (inserts a `long int` as a UTF-8 byte sequence).

Unlike other push functions, this function checks for the stack space it needs, including the slot for its result.

lua_pushglobaltable

```
void lua_pushglobaltable (lua_State *L);
```
[-0, +1, –]

Pushes the global environment onto the stack.

lua_pushinteger

```
void lua_pushinteger (lua_State *L, lua_Integer n);
```
[-0, +1, –]

Pushes an integer with value n onto the stack.

lua_pushlightuserdata

```
void lua_pushlightuserdata (lua_State *L, void *p);
```
[-0, +1, –]

Pushes a light userdata onto the stack.

Userdata represent C values in Lua. A *light userdata* represents a pointer, a void*. It is a value (like a number): you do not create it, it has no individual metatable, and it is not collected (as it was never created). A light userdata is equal to "any" light userdata with the same C address.

lua_pushliteral

```
const char *lua_pushliteral (lua_State *L, const char *s);
```
[-0, +1, *m*]

This macro is equivalent to `lua_pushstring`, but should be used only when s is a literal string.

lua_pushlstring

```
const char *lua_pushlstring (lua_State *L, const char *s, size_t len);
```
[-0, +1, *m*]

Pushes the string pointed to by s with size `len` onto the stack. Lua makes (or reuses) an internal copy of the given string, so the memory at s can be freed or reused immediately after the function returns. The string can contain any binary data, including embedded zeros.

Returns a pointer to the internal copy of the string.

lua_pushnil

```
void lua_pushnil (lua_State *L);
```
[-0, +1, –]

Pushes a nil value onto the stack.

lua_pushnumber

```
void lua_pushnumber (lua_State *L, lua_Number n);
```
[-0, +1, –]

Pushes a float with value n onto the stack.

lua_pushstring

```
const char *lua_pushstring (lua_State *L, const char *s);
```
[-0, +1, *m*]

Pushes the zero-terminated string pointed to by s onto the stack. Lua makes (or reuses) an internal copy of the given string, so the memory at s can be freed or reused immediately after the function returns.

Returns a pointer to the internal copy of the string.

If s is NULL, pushes **nil** and returns NULL.

lua_pushthread

```
int lua_pushthread (lua_State *L);
```
[-0, +1, –]

Pushes the thread represented by L onto the stack. Returns 1 if this thread is the main thread of its state.

lua_pushvalue

```
void lua_pushvalue (lua_State *L, int index);                              [-0, +1, -]
```

Pushes a copy of the element at the given index onto the stack.

lua_pushvfstring

```
const char *lua_pushvfstring (lua_State *L,                                [-0, +1, m]
                             const char *fmt,
                             va_list argp);
```

Equivalent to `lua_pushfstring`, except that it receives a `va_list` instead of a variable number of arguments.

lua_rawequal

```
int lua_rawequal (lua_State *L, int index1, int index2);                   [-0, +0, -]
```

Returns 1 if the two values in indices `index1` and `index2` are primitively equal (that is, without calling the __eq metamethod). Otherwise returns 0. Also returns 0 if any of the indices are not valid.

lua_rawget

```
int lua_rawget (lua_State *L, int index);                                  [-1, +1, -]
```

Similar to `lua_gettable`, but does a raw access (i.e., without metamethods).

lua_rawgeti

```
int lua_rawgeti (lua_State *L, int index, lua_Integer n);                  [-0, +1, -]
```

Pushes onto the stack the value `t[n]`, where `t` is the table at the given index. The access is raw, that is, it does not invoke the __index metamethod.

Returns the type of the pushed value.

lua_rawgetp

```
int lua_rawgetp (lua_State *L, int index, const void *p);                  [-0, +1, -]
```

Pushes onto the stack the value `t[k]`, where `t` is the table at the given index and k is the pointer p represented as a light userdata. The access is raw; that is, it does not invoke the __index metamethod.

Returns the type of the pushed value.

lua_rawlen

```
size_t lua_rawlen (lua_State *L, int index);                               [-0, +0, -]
```

Returns the raw "length" of the value at the given index: for strings, this is the string length; for tables, this is the result of the length operator ('#') with no metamethods; for userdata, this is the size of the block of memory allocated for the userdata; for other values, it is 0.

lua_rawset

```
void lua_rawset (lua_State *L, int index);                                 [-2, +0, m]
```

Similar to `lua_settable`, but does a raw assignment (i.e., without metamethods).

lua_rawseti

```
void lua_rawseti (lua_State *L, int index, lua_Integer i);
```
[-1, +0, *m*]

Does the equivalent of t[i] = v, where t is the table at the given index and v is the value at the top of the stack.

This function pops the value from the stack. The assignment is raw, that is, it does not invoke the __newindex metamethod.

lua_rawsetp

```
void lua_rawsetp (lua_State *L, int index, const void *p);
```
[-1, +0, *m*]

Does the equivalent of t[p] = v, where t is the table at the given index, p is encoded as a light userdata, and v is the value at the top of the stack.

This function pops the value from the stack. The assignment is raw, that is, it does not invoke __newindex metamethod.

lua_Reader

```
typedef const char * (*lua_Reader) (lua_State *L,
                                    void *data,
                                    size_t *size);
```

The reader function used by lua_load. Every time it needs another piece of the chunk, lua_load calls the reader, passing along its data parameter. The reader must return a pointer to a block of memory with a new piece of the chunk and set size to the block size. The block must exist until the reader function is called again. To signal the end of the chunk, the reader must return NULL or set size to zero. The reader function may return pieces of any size greater than zero.

lua_register

```
void lua_register (lua_State *L, const char *name, lua_CFunction f);
```
[-0, +0, *e*]

Sets the C function f as the new value of global name. It is defined as a macro:

```
#define lua_register(L,n,f) \
        (lua_pushcfunction(L, f), lua_setglobal(L, n))
```

lua_remove

```
void lua_remove (lua_State *L, int index);
```
[-1, +0, –]

Removes the element at the given valid index, shifting down the elements above this index to fill the gap. This function cannot be called with a pseudo-index, because a pseudo-index is not an actual stack position.

lua_replace

```
void lua_replace (lua_State *L, int index);
```
[-1, +0, –]

Moves the top element into the given valid index without shifting any element (therefore replacing the value at that given index), and then pops the top element.

lua_resume

```
int lua_resume (lua_State *L, lua_State *from, int nargs);                    [-?, +?, –]
```

Starts and resumes a coroutine in the given thread L.

To start a coroutine, you push onto the thread stack the main function plus any arguments; then you call `lua_resume`, with `nargs` being the number of arguments. This call returns when the coroutine suspends or finishes its execution. When it returns, the stack contains all values passed to `lua_yield`, or all values returned by the body function. `lua_resume` returns `LUA_YIELD` if the coroutine yields, `LUA_OK` if the coroutine finishes its execution without errors, or an error code in case of errors (see `lua_pcall`).

In case of errors, the stack is not unwound, so you can use the debug API over it. The error object is on the top of the stack.

To resume a coroutine, you remove any results from the last `lua_yield`, put on its stack only the values to be passed as results from `yield`, and then call `lua_resume`.

The parameter `from` represents the coroutine that is resuming L. If there is no such coroutine, this parameter can be `NULL`.

lua_rotate

```
void lua_rotate (lua_State *L, int idx, int n);                              [-0, +0, –]
```

Rotates the stack elements between the valid index `idx` and the top of the stack. The elements are rotated n positions in the direction of the top, for a positive n, or -n positions in the direction of the bottom, for a negative n. The absolute value of n must not be greater than the size of the slice being rotated. This function cannot be called with a pseudo-index, because a pseudo-index is not an actual stack position.

lua_setallocf

```
void lua_setallocf (lua_State *L, lua_Alloc f, void *ud);                    [-0, +0, –]
```

Changes the allocator function of a given state to f with user data ud.

lua_setfield

```
void lua_setfield (lua_State *L, int index, const char *k);                  [-1, +0, e]
```

Does the equivalent to t[k] = v, where t is the value at the given index and v is the value at the top of the stack.

This function pops the value from the stack. As in Lua, this function may trigger a metamethod for the "newindex" event (see §2.4).

lua_setglobal

```
void lua_setglobal (lua_State *L, const char *name);                         [-1, +0, e]
```

Pops a value from the stack and sets it as the new value of global name.

lua_seti

```
void lua_seti (lua_State *L, int index, lua_Integer n);                      [-1, +0, e]
```

Does the equivalent to t[n] = v, where t is the value at the given index and v is the value at the top of the stack.

This function pops the value from the stack. As in Lua, this function may trigger a metamethod for the "newindex" event (see §2.4).

lua_setmetatable

```
void lua_setmetatable (lua_State *L, int index);
```
[-1, +0, –]

Pops a table from the stack and sets it as the new metatable for the value at the given index.

lua_settable

```
void lua_settable (lua_State *L, int index);
```
[-2, +0, e]

Does the equivalent to t[k] = v, where t is the value at the given index, v is the value at the top of the stack, and k is the value just below the top.

This function pops both the key and the value from the stack. As in Lua, this function may trigger a metamethod for the "newindex" event (see §2.4).

lua_settop

```
void lua_settop (lua_State *L, int index);
```
[-?, +?, –]

Accepts any index, or 0, and sets the stack top to this index. If the new top is larger than the old one, then the new elements are filled with **nil**. If index is 0, then all stack elements are removed.

lua_setuservalue

```
void lua_setuservalue (lua_State *L, int index);
```
[-1, +0, –]

Pops a value from the stack and sets it as the new value associated to the userdata at the given index.

lua_State

```
typedef struct lua_State lua_State;
```

An opaque structure that points to a thread and indirectly (through the thread) to the whole state of a Lua interpreter. The Lua library is fully reentrant: it has no global variables. All information about a state is accessible through this structure.

A pointer to this structure must be passed as the first argument to every function in the library, except to lua_newstate, which creates a Lua state from scratch.

lua_status

```
int lua_status (lua_State *L);
```
[-0, +0, –]

Returns the status of the thread L.

The status can be 0 (LUA_OK) for a normal thread, an error code if the thread finished the execution of a lua_resume with an error, or LUA_YIELD if the thread is suspended.

You can only call functions in threads with status LUA_OK. You can resume threads with status LUA_OK (to start a new coroutine) or LUA_YIELD (to resume a coroutine).

lua_stringtonumber

[-0, +1, –]

```
size_t lua_stringtonumber (lua_State *L, const char *s);
```

Converts the zero-terminated string s to a number, pushes that number into the stack, and returns the total size of the string, that is, its length plus one. The conversion can result in an integer or a float, according to the lexical conventions of Lua (see §3.1). The string may have leading and trailing spaces and a sign. If the string is not a valid numeral, returns 0 and pushes nothing. (Note that the result can be used as a boolean, true if the conversion succeeds.)

lua_toboolean

```
int lua_toboolean (lua_State *L, int index);
```
[-0, +0, –]

Converts the Lua value at the given index to a C boolean value (0 or 1). Like all tests in Lua, lua_toboolean returns true for any Lua value different from **false** and **nil**; otherwise it returns false. (If you want to accept only actual boolean values, use lua_isboolean to test the value's type.)

lua_tocfunction

```
lua_CFunction lua_tocfunction (lua_State *L, int index);
```
[-0, +0, –]

Converts a value at the given index to a C function. That value must be a C function; otherwise, returns NULL.

lua_tointeger

```
lua_Integer lua_tointeger (lua_State *L, int index);
```
[-0, +0, –]

Equivalent to lua_tointegerx with isnum equal to NULL.

lua_tointegerx

```
lua_Integer lua_tointegerx (lua_State *L, int index, int *isnum);
```
[-0, +0, –]

Converts the Lua value at the given index to the signed integral type lua_Integer. The Lua value must be an integer, or a number or string convertible to an integer (see §3.4.3); otherwise, lua_tointegerx returns 0.

If isnum is not NULL, its referent is assigned a boolean value that indicates whether the operation succeeded.

lua_tolstring

```
const char *lua_tolstring (lua_State *L, int index, size_t *len);
```
[-0, +0, m]

Converts the Lua value at the given index to a C string. If len is not NULL, it sets *len with the string length. The Lua value must be a string or a number; otherwise, the function returns NULL. If the value is a number, then lua_tolstring also *changes the actual value in the stack to a string*. (This change confuses lua_next when lua_tolstring is applied to keys during a table traversal.)

lua_tolstring returns a pointer to a string inside the Lua state. This string always has a zero ('\0') after its last character (as in C), but can contain other zeros in its body.

Because Lua has garbage collection, there is no guarantee that the pointer returned by lua_tolstring will be valid after the corresponding Lua value is removed from the stack.

lua_tonumber

[-0, +0, –]

```
lua_Number lua_tonumber (lua_State *L, int index);
```

Equivalent to `lua_tonumberx` with `isnum` equal to `NULL`.

lua_tonumberx

```
lua_Number lua_tonumberx (lua_State *L, int index, int *isnum);
```
[-0, +0, –]

Converts the Lua value at the given index to the C type `lua_Number` (see `lua_Number`). The Lua value must be a number or a string convertible to a number (see §3.4.3); otherwise, `lua_tonumberx` returns 0.

If `isnum` is not `NULL`, its referent is assigned a boolean value that indicates whether the operation succeeded.

lua_topointer

```
const void *lua_topointer (lua_State *L, int index);
```
[-0, +0, –]

Converts the value at the given index to a generic C pointer (`void*`). The value can be a userdata, a table, a thread, or a function; otherwise, `lua_topointer` returns `NULL`. Different objects will give different pointers. There is no way to convert the pointer back to its original value.

Typically this function is used only for hashing and debug information.

lua_tostring

```
const char *lua_tostring (lua_State *L, int index);
```
[-0, +0, *m*]

Equivalent to `lua_tolstring` with `len` equal to `NULL`.

lua_tothread

```
lua_State *lua_tothread (lua_State *L, int index);
```
[-0, +0, –]

Converts the value at the given index to a Lua thread (represented as `lua_State*`). This value must be a thread; otherwise, the function returns `NULL`.

lua_touserdata

```
void *lua_touserdata (lua_State *L, int index);
```
[-0, +0, –]

If the value at the given index is a full userdata, returns its block address. If the value is a light userdata, returns its pointer. Otherwise, returns `NULL`.

lua_type

```
int lua_type (lua_State *L, int index);
```
[-0, +0, –]

Returns the type of the value in the given valid index, or `LUA_TNONE` for a non-valid (but acceptable) index. The types returned by `lua_type` are coded by the following constants defined in `lua.h`: `LUA_TNIL` (0), `LUA_TNUMBER`, `LUA_TBOOLEAN`, `LUA_TSTRING`, `LUA_TTABLE`, `LUA_TFUNCTION`, `LUA_TUSERDATA`, `LUA_TTHREAD`, and `LUA_TLIGHTUSERDATA`.

lua_typename

```
const char *lua_typename (lua_State *L, int tp);
```
[-0, +0, –]

Returns the name of the type encoded by the value `tp`, which must be one the values returned by `lua_type`.

lua_Unsigned

```
typedef ... lua_Unsigned;
```

The unsigned version of `lua_Integer`.

lua_upvalueindex

```
int lua_upvalueindex (int i);
```
[-0, +0, –]

Returns the pseudo-index that represents the i-th upvalue of the running function (see §4.4).

lua_version

```
const lua_Number *lua_version (lua_State *L);
```
[-0, +0, –]

Returns the address of the version number (a C static variable) stored in the Lua core. When called with a valid `lua_State`, returns the address of the version used to create that state. When called with `NULL`, returns the address of the version running the call.

lua_Writer

```
typedef int (*lua_Writer) (lua_State *L,
                           const void* p,
                           size_t sz,
                           void* ud);
```

The type of the writer function used by `lua_dump`. Every time it produces another piece of chunk, `lua_dump` calls the writer, passing along the buffer to be written (p), its size (sz), and the data parameter supplied to `lua_dump`.

The writer returns an error code: 0 means no errors; any other value means an error and stops `lua_dump` from calling the writer again.

lua_xmove

```
void lua_xmove (lua_State *from, lua_State *to, int n);
```
[-?, +?, –]

Exchange values between different threads of the same state.

This function pops n values from the stack `from`, and pushes them onto the stack `to`.

lua_yield

```
int lua_yield (lua_State *L, int nresults);
```
[-?, +?, e]

This function is equivalent to `lua_yieldk`, but it has no continuation (see §4.7). Therefore, when the thread resumes, it continues the function that called the function calling `lua_yield`.

lua_yieldk

```
int lua_yieldk (lua_State *L,
                int nresults,
                lua_KContext ctx,
                lua_KFunction k);
```
[-?, +?, e]

Yields a coroutine (thread).

When a C function calls `lua_yieldk`, the running coroutine suspends its execution, and the call to `lua_resume` that started this coroutine returns. The parameter `nresults` is the number of values from the stack that will be passed as results to `lua_resume`.

When the coroutine is resumed again, Lua calls the given continuation function k to continue the execution of the C function that yielded (see §4.7). This continuation function receives the same stack from the previous function, with the n results removed and replaced by the arguments passed to `lua_resume`. Moreover, the continuation function receives the value `ctx` that was passed to `lua_yieldk`.

Usually, this function does not return; when the coroutine eventually resumes, it continues executing the continuation function. However, there is one special case, which is when this function is called from inside a line or a count hook (see §4.9). In that case, `lua_yieldk` should be called with no continuation (probably in the form of `lua_yield`) and no results, and the hook should return immediately after the call. Lua will yield and, when the coroutine resumes again, it will continue the normal execution of the (Lua) function that triggered the hook.

This function can raise an error if it is called from a thread with a pending C call with no continuation function, or it is called from a thread that is not running inside a resume (e.g., the main thread).

4.9 – The Debug Interface

Lua has no built-in debugging facilities. Instead, it offers a special interface by means of functions and *hooks*. This interface allows the construction of different kinds of debuggers, profilers, and other tools that need "inside information" from the interpreter.

lua_Debug

```
typedef struct lua_Debug {
  int event;
  const char *name;           /* (n) */
  const char *namewhat;       /* (n) */
  const char *what;           /* (S) */
  const char *source;         /* (S) */
  int currentline;            /* (l) */
  int linedefined;            /* (S) */
  int lastlinedefined;        /* (S) */
  unsigned char nups;         /* (u) number of upvalues */
  unsigned char nparams;      /* (u) number of parameters */
  char isvararg;              /* (u) */
  char istailcall;            /* (t) */
  char short_src[LUA_IDSIZE]; /* (S) */
  /* private part */
  other fields
} lua_Debug;
```

A structure used to carry different pieces of information about a function or an activation record. `lua_getstack` fills only the private part of this structure, for later use. To fill the other fields of `lua_Debug` with useful information, call `lua_getinfo`.

The fields of `lua_Debug` have the following meaning:

> **source:** the name of the chunk that created the function. If `source` starts with a '@', it means that the function was defined in a file where the file name follows the '@'. If `source` starts with a '=', the remainder of its contents describe the source in a user-dependent manner. Otherwise, the function was defined in a string where `source` is that string.

short_src: a "printable" version of `source`, to be used in error messages.

linedefined: the line number where the definition of the function starts.

lastlinedefined: the line number where the definition of the function ends.

what: the string `"Lua"` if the function is a Lua function, `"C"` if it is a C function, `"main"` if it is the main part of a chunk.

currentline: the current line where the given function is executing. When no line information is available, `currentline` is set to -1.

name: a reasonable name for the given function. Because functions in Lua are first-class values, they do not have a fixed name: some functions can be the value of multiple global variables, while others can be stored only in a table field. The `lua_getinfo` function checks how the function was called to find a suitable name. If it cannot find a name, then `name` is set to NULL.

namewhat: explains the `name` field. The value of `namewhat` can be `"global"`, `"local"`, `"method"`, `"field"`, `"upvalue"`, or `""` (the empty string), according to how the function was called. (Lua uses the empty string when no other option seems to apply.)

istailcall: true if this function invocation was called by a tail call. In this case, the caller of this level is not in the stack.

nups: the number of upvalues of the function.

nparams: the number of fixed parameters of the function (always 0 for C functions).

isvararg: true if the function is a vararg function (always true for C functions).

lua_gethook

```
lua_Hook lua_gethook (lua_State *L);
```
[-0, +0, –]

Returns the current hook function.

lua_gethookcount

```
int lua_gethookcount (lua_State *L);
```
[-0, +0, –]

Returns the current hook count.

lua_gethookmask

```
int lua_gethookmask (lua_State *L);
```
[-0, +0, –]

Returns the current hook mask.

lua_getinfo

```
int lua_getinfo (lua_State *L, const char *what, lua_Debug *ar);
```
[-(0|1), +(0|1|2), e]

Gets information about a specific function or function invocation.

To get information about a function invocation, the parameter `ar` must be a valid activation record that was filled by a previous call to `lua_getstack` or given as argument to a hook (see `lua_Hook`).

To get information about a function you push it onto the stack and start the `what` string with the character `'>'`. (In that case, `lua_getinfo` pops the function from the top of the stack.) For instance, to know in which line a function `f` was defined, you can write the following code:

```
lua_Debug ar;
lua_getglobal(L, "f");  /* get global 'f' */
lua_getinfo(L, ">S", &ar);
printf("%d\n", ar.linedefined);
```

Each character in the string `what` selects some fields of the structure `ar` to be filled or a value to be pushed on the stack:

> **'n'**: fills in the field `name` and `namewhat`;
> **'S'**: fills in the fields `source`, `short_src`, `linedefined`, `lastlinedefined`, and `what`;
> **'l'**: fills in the field `currentline`;
> **'t'**: fills in the field `istailcall`;
> **'u'**: fills in the fields `nups`, `nparams`, and `isvararg`;
> **'f'**: pushes onto the stack the function that is running at the given level;
> **'L'**: pushes onto the stack a table whose indices are the numbers of the lines that are valid on the function. (A *valid line* is a line with some associated code, that is, a line where you can put a break point. Non-valid lines include empty lines and comments.)

If this option is given together with option 'f', its table is pushed after the function.

This function returns 0 on error (for instance, an invalid option in `what`).

lua_getlocal

```
const char *lua_getlocal (lua_State *L, const lua_Debug *ar, int n);
```
[-0, +(0|1), –]

Gets information about a local variable of a given activation record or a given function.

In the first case, the parameter `ar` must be a valid activation record that was filled by a previous call to `lua_getstack` or given as argument to a hook (see `lua_Hook`). The index n selects which local variable to inspect; see `debug.getlocal` for details about variable indices and names.

`lua_getlocal` pushes the variable's value onto the stack and returns its name.

In the second case, `ar` must be `NULL` and the function to be inspected must be at the top of the stack. In this case, only parameters of Lua functions are visible (as there is no information about what variables are active) and no values are pushed onto the stack.

Returns `NULL` (and pushes nothing) when the index is greater than the number of active local variables.

lua_getstack

```
int lua_getstack (lua_State *L, int level, lua_Debug *ar);
```
[-0, +0, –]

Gets information about the interpreter runtime stack.

This function fills parts of a `lua_Debug` structure with an identification of the *activation record* of the function executing at a given level. Level 0 is the current running function, whereas level *n+1* is the function that has called level *n* (except for tail calls, which do not count on the stack). When there are no errors, `lua_getstack` returns 1; when called with a level greater than the stack depth, it returns 0.

lua_getupvalue

```
const char *lua_getupvalue (lua_State *L, int funcindex, int n);
```
[-0, +(0|1), –]

Gets information about the n-th upvalue of the closure at index `funcindex`. It pushes the upvalue's value onto the stack and returns its name. Returns `NULL` (and pushes nothing) when the index n is greater than the number of upvalues.

For C functions, this function uses the empty string "" as a name for all upvalues. (For Lua functions, upvalues are the external local variables that the function uses, and that are consequently included in its closure.)

Upvalues have no particular order, as they are active through the whole function. They are numbered in an arbitrary order.

lua_Hook

```
typedef void (*lua_Hook) (lua_State *L, lua_Debug *ar);
```

Type for debugging hook functions.

Whenever a hook is called, its `ar` argument has its field `event` set to the specific event that triggered the hook. Lua identifies these events with the following constants: `LUA_HOOKCALL`, `LUA_HOOKRET`, `LUA_HOOKTAILCALL`, `LUA_HOOKLINE`, and `LUA_HOOKCOUNT`. Moreover, for line events, the field `currentline` is also set. To get the value of any other field in `ar`, the hook must call `lua_getinfo`.

For call events, `event` can be `LUA_HOOKCALL`, the normal value, or `LUA_HOOKTAILCALL`, for a tail call; in this case, there will be no corresponding return event.

While Lua is running a hook, it disables other calls to hooks. Therefore, if a hook calls back Lua to execute a function or a chunk, this execution occurs without any calls to hooks.

Hook functions cannot have continuations, that is, they cannot call `lua_yieldk`, `lua_pcallk`, or `lua_callk` with a non-null k.

Hook functions can yield under the following conditions: Only count and line events can yield; to yield, a hook function must finish its execution calling `lua_yield` with `nresults` equal to zero (that is, with no values).

lua_sethook

```
void lua_sethook (lua_State *L, lua_Hook f, int mask, int count);          [-0, +0, –]
```

Sets the debugging hook function.

Argument `f` is the hook function. `mask` specifies on which events the hook will be called: it is formed by a bitwise OR of the constants `LUA_MASKCALL`, `LUA_MASKRET`, `LUA_MASKLINE`, and `LUA_MASKCOUNT`. The `count` argument is only meaningful when the mask includes `LUA_MASKCOUNT`. For each event, the hook is called as explained below:

> **The call hook:** is called when the interpreter calls a function. The hook is called just after Lua enters the new function, before the function gets its arguments.
> **The return hook:** is called when the interpreter returns from a function. The hook is called just before Lua leaves the function. There is no standard way to access the values to be returned by the function.
> **The line hook:** is called when the interpreter is about to start the execution of a new line of code, or when it jumps back in the code (even to the same line). (This event only happens while Lua is executing a Lua function.)
> **The count hook:** is called after the interpreter executes every `count` instructions. (This event only happens while Lua is executing a Lua function.)

A hook is disabled by setting `mask` to zero.

lua_setlocal

```
const char *lua_setlocal (lua_State *L, const lua_Debug *ar, int n);     [-(0|1), +0, –]
```

Sets the value of a local variable of a given activation record. It assigns the value at the top of the stack to the variable and returns its name. It also pops the value from the stack.

Returns NULL (and pops nothing) when the index is greater than the number of active local variables.

Parameters `ar` and `n` are as in function `lua_getlocal`.

lua_setupvalue

```
const char *lua_setupvalue (lua_State *L, int funcindex, int n);    [-(0|1), +0, -]
```

Sets the value of a closure's upvalue. It assigns the value at the top of the stack to the upvalue and returns its name. It also pops the value from the stack.

Returns NULL (and pops nothing) when the index n is greater than the number of upvalues.

Parameters `funcindex` and `n` are as in function `lua_getupvalue`.

lua_upvalueid

```
void *lua_upvalueid (lua_State *L, int funcindex, int n);    [-0, +0, -]
```

Returns a unique identifier for the upvalue numbered n from the closure at index `funcindex`.

These unique identifiers allow a program to check whether different closures share upvalues. Lua closures that share an upvalue (that is, that access a same external local variable) will return identical ids for those upvalue indices.

Parameters `funcindex` and `n` are as in function `lua_getupvalue`, but n cannot be greater than the number of upvalues.

lua_upvaluejoin

```
void lua_upvaluejoin (lua_State *L, int funcindex1, int n1,    [-0, +0, -]
                                    int funcindex2, int n2);
```

Make the n1-th upvalue of the Lua closure at index `funcindex1` refer to the n2-th upvalue of the Lua closure at index `funcindex2`.

5 – The Auxiliary Library

The *auxiliary library* provides several convenient functions to interface C with Lua. While the basic API provides the primitive functions for all interactions between C and Lua, the auxiliary library provides higher-level functions for some common tasks.

All functions and types from the auxiliary library are defined in header file `lauxlib.h` and have a prefix `luaL_`.

All functions in the auxiliary library are built on top of the basic API, and so they provide nothing that cannot be done with that API. Nevertheless, the use of the auxiliary library ensures more consistency to your code.

Several functions in the auxiliary library use internally some extra stack slots. When a function in the auxiliary library uses less than five slots, it does not check the stack size; it simply assumes that there are enough slots.

Several functions in the auxiliary library are used to check C function arguments. Because the error message is formatted for arguments (e.g., `"bad argument #1"`), you should not use these functions for other stack values.

Functions called `luaL_check*` always raise an error if the check is not satisfied.

5.1 – Functions and Types

Here we list all functions and types from the auxiliary library in alphabetical order.

luaL_addchar

```
void luaL_addchar (luaL_Buffer *B, char c);
```
[-?, +?, *m*]

Adds the byte c to the buffer B (see `luaL_Buffer`).

luaL_addlstring

```
void luaL_addlstring (luaL_Buffer *B, const char *s, size_t l);
```
[-?, +?, *m*]

Adds the string pointed to by s with length l to the buffer B (see `luaL_Buffer`). The string can contain embedded zeros.

luaL_addsize

```
void luaL_addsize (luaL_Buffer *B, size_t n);
```
[-?, +?, –]

Adds to the buffer B (see `luaL_Buffer`) a string of length n previously copied to the buffer area (see `luaL_prepbuffer`).

luaL_addstring

```
void luaL_addstring (luaL_Buffer *B, const char *s);
```
[-?, +?, *m*]

Adds the zero-terminated string pointed to by s to the buffer B (see `luaL_Buffer`).

luaL_addvalue

```
void luaL_addvalue (luaL_Buffer *B);
```
[-1, +?, *m*]

Adds the value at the top of the stack to the buffer B (see `luaL_Buffer`). Pops the value.

This is the only function on string buffers that can (and must) be called with an extra element on the stack, which is the value to be added to the buffer.

luaL_argcheck

```
void luaL_argcheck (lua_State *L,
                    int cond,
                    int arg,
                    const char *extramsg);
```
[-0, +0, *v*]

Checks whether cond is true. If it is not, raises an error with a standard message (see `luaL_argerror`).

luaL_argerror

```
int luaL_argerror (lua_State *L, int arg, const char *extramsg);
```
[-0, +0, *v*]

Raises an error reporting a problem with argument arg of the C function that called it, using a standard message that includes extramsg as a comment:

    bad argument #*arg* to '*funcname*' (*extramsg*)

This function never returns.

luaL_Buffer

```
typedef struct luaL_Buffer luaL_Buffer;
```

Type for a *string buffer*.

A string buffer allows C code to build Lua strings piecemeal. Its pattern of use is as follows:

> First declare a variable b of type `luaL_Buffer`.
> Then initialize it with a call `luaL_buffinit(L, &b)`.
> Then add string pieces to the buffer calling any of the `luaL_add*` functions.
> Finish by calling `luaL_pushresult(&b)`. This call leaves the final string on the top of the stack.

If you know beforehand the total size of the resulting string, you can use the buffer like this:

> First declare a variable b of type `luaL_Buffer`.
> Then initialize it and preallocate a space of size sz with a call `luaL_buffinitsize(L, &b, sz)`.
> Then copy the string into that space.
> Finish by calling `luaL_pushresultsize(&b, sz)`, where sz is the total size of the resulting string copied into that space.

During its normal operation, a string buffer uses a variable number of stack slots. So, while using a buffer, you cannot assume that you know where the top of the stack is. You can use the stack between successive calls to buffer operations as long as that use is balanced; that is, when you call a buffer operation, the stack is at the same level it was immediately after the previous buffer operation. (The only exception to this rule is `luaL_addvalue`.) After calling `luaL_pushresult` the stack is back to its level when the buffer was initialized, plus the final string on its top.

luaL_buffinit

```
void luaL_buffinit (lua_State *L, luaL_Buffer *B);                          [-0, +0, –]
```

Initializes a buffer B. This function does not allocate any space; the buffer must be declared as a variable (see luaL_Buffer).

luaL_buffinitsize

```
char *luaL_buffinitsize (lua_State *L, luaL_Buffer *B, size_t sz);          [-?, +?, m]
```

Equivalent to the sequence luaL_buffinit, luaL_prepbuffsize.

luaL_callmeta

```
int luaL_callmeta (lua_State *L, int obj, const char *e);                   [-0, +(0|1), e]
```

Calls a metamethod.

If the object at index obj has a metatable and this metatable has a field e, this function calls this field passing the object as its only argument. In this case this function returns true and pushes onto the stack the value returned by the call. If there is no metatable or no metamethod, this function returns false (without pushing any value on the stack).

luaL_checkany

```
void luaL_checkany (lua_State *L, int arg);                                 [-0, +0, v]
```

Checks whether the function has an argument of any type (including **nil**) at position arg.

luaL_checkinteger

```
lua_Integer luaL_checkinteger (lua_State *L, int arg);                      [-0, +0, v]
```

Checks whether the function argument arg is an integer (or can be converted to an integer) and returns this integer cast to a lua_Integer.

luaL_checklstring

```
const char *luaL_checklstring (lua_State *L, int arg, size_t *l);           [-0, +0, v]
```

Checks whether the function argument arg is a string and returns this string; if l is not NULL fills *l with the string's length.

This function uses lua_tolstring to get its result, so all conversions and caveats of that function apply here.

luaL_checknumber

```
lua_Number luaL_checknumber (lua_State *L, int arg);                        [-0, +0, v]
```

Checks whether the function argument arg is a number and returns this number.

luaL_checkoption

```
int luaL_checkoption (lua_State *L,                                         [-0, +0, v]
                      int arg,
                      const char *def,
                      const char *const lst[]);
```

Checks whether the function argument `arg` is a string and searches for this string in the array `lst` (which must be NULL-terminated). Returns the index in the array where the string was found. Raises an error if the argument is not a string or if the string cannot be found.

If `def` is not `NULL`, the function uses `def` as a default value when there is no argument `arg` or when this argument is **nil**.

This is a useful function for mapping strings to C enums. (The usual convention in Lua libraries is to use strings instead of numbers to select options.)

luaL_checkstack

```
void luaL_checkstack (lua_State *L, int sz, const char *msg);
```
[-0, +0, v]

Grows the stack size to `top + sz` elements, raising an error if the stack cannot grow to that size. `msg` is an additional text to go into the error message (or `NULL` for no additional text).

luaL_checkstring

```
const char *luaL_checkstring (lua_State *L, int arg);
```
[-0, +0, v]

Checks whether the function argument `arg` is a string and returns this string.

This function uses `lua_tolstring` to get its result, so all conversions and caveats of that function apply here.

luaL_checktype

```
void luaL_checktype (lua_State *L, int arg, int t);
```
[-0, +0, v]

Checks whether the function argument `arg` has type t. See `lua_type` for the encoding of types for t.

luaL_checkudata

```
void *luaL_checkudata (lua_State *L, int arg, const char *tname);
```
[-0, +0, v]

Checks whether the function argument `arg` is a userdata of the type `tname` (see `luaL_newmetatable`) and returns the userdata address (see `lua_touserdata`).

luaL_checkversion

```
void luaL_checkversion (lua_State *L);
```
[-0, +0, v]

Checks whether the core running the call, the core that created the Lua state, and the code making the call are all using the same version of Lua. Also checks whether the core running the call and the core that created the Lua state are using the same address space.

luaL_dofile

```
int luaL_dofile (lua_State *L, const char *filename);
```
[-0, +?, e]

Loads and runs the given file. It is defined as the following macro:

```
(luaL_loadfile(L, filename) || lua_pcall(L, 0, LUA_MULTRET, 0))
```

It returns false if there are no errors or true in case of errors.

luaL_dostring

```
int luaL_dostring (lua_State *L, const char *str);
```
[-0, +?, –]

Loads and runs the given string. It is defined as the following macro:

```
(luaL_loadstring(L, str) || lua_pcall(L, 0, LUA_MULTRET, 0))
```

It returns false if there are no errors or true in case of errors.

luaL_error

```
int luaL_error (lua_State *L, const char *fmt, ...);
```
[-0, +0, v]

Raises an error. The error message format is given by fmt plus any extra arguments, following the same rules of `lua_pushfstring`. It also adds at the beginning of the message the file name and the line number where the error occurred, if this information is available.

This function never returns, but it is an idiom to use it in C functions as return luaL_error(*args*).

luaL_execresult

```
int luaL_execresult (lua_State *L, int stat);
```
[-0, +3, m]

This function produces the return values for process-related functions in the standard library (`os.execute` and `io.close`).

luaL_fileresult

```
int luaL_fileresult (lua_State *L, int stat, const char *fname);
```
[-0, +(1|3), m]

This function produces the return values for file-related functions in the standard library (`io.open`, `os.rename`, `file:seek`, etc.).

luaL_getmetafield

```
int luaL_getmetafield (lua_State *L, int obj, const char *e);
```
[-0, +(0|1), m]

Pushes onto the stack the field e from the metatable of the object at index obj and returns the type of pushed value. If the object does not have a metatable, or if the metatable does not have this field, pushes nothing and returns LUA_TNIL.

luaL_getmetatable

```
int luaL_getmetatable (lua_State *L, const char *tname);
```
[-0, +1, m]

Pushes onto the stack the metatable associated with name tname in the registry (see `luaL_newmetatable`) (**nil** if there is no metatable associated with that name). Returns the type of the pushed value.

luaL_getsubtable

```
int luaL_getsubtable (lua_State *L, int idx, const char *fname);
```
[-0, +1, e]

Ensures that the value t[fname], where t is the value at index idx, is a table, and pushes that table onto the stack. Returns true if it finds a previous table there and false if it creates a new table.

luaL_gsub

[-0, +1, m]

```
const char *luaL_gsub (lua_State *L,
                       const char *s,
                       const char *p,
                       const char *r);
```

Creates a copy of string s by replacing any occurrence of the string p with the string r. Pushes the resulting string on the stack and returns it.

luaL_len

```
lua_Integer luaL_len (lua_State *L, int index);
```
[-0, +0, *e*]

Returns the "length" of the value at the given index as a number; it is equivalent to the '#' operator in Lua (see §3.4.7). Raises an error if the result of the operation is not an integer. (This case only can happen through metamethods.)

luaL_loadbuffer

```
int luaL_loadbuffer (lua_State *L,
                     const char *buff,
                     size_t sz,
                     const char *name);
```
[-0, +1, –]

Equivalent to `luaL_loadbufferx` with mode equal to NULL.

luaL_loadbufferx

```
int luaL_loadbufferx (lua_State *L,
                      const char *buff,
                      size_t sz,
                      const char *name,
                      const char *mode);
```
[-0, +1, –]

Loads a buffer as a Lua chunk. This function uses `lua_load` to load the chunk in the buffer pointed to by `buff` with size `sz`.

This function returns the same results as `lua_load`. name is the chunk name, used for debug information and error messages. The string mode works as in function `lua_load`.

luaL_loadfile

```
int luaL_loadfile (lua_State *L, const char *filename);
```
[-0, +1, *m*]

Equivalent to `luaL_loadfilex` with mode equal to NULL.

luaL_loadfilex

```
int luaL_loadfilex (lua_State *L, const char *filename,
                                  const char *mode);
```
[-0, +1, *m*]

Loads a file as a Lua chunk. This function uses `lua_load` to load the chunk in the file named `filename`. If `filename` is NULL, then it loads from the standard input. The first line in the file is ignored if it starts with a #.

The string mode works as in function `lua_load`.

This function returns the same results as `lua_load`, but it has an extra error code LUA_ERRFILE if it cannot open/read the file or the file has a wrong mode.

As `lua_load`, this function only loads the chunk; it does not run it.

luaL_loadstring

`int luaL_loadstring (lua_State *L, const char *s);` [-0, +1, –]

Loads a string as a Lua chunk. This function uses `lua_load` to load the chunk in the zero-terminated string s.

This function returns the same results as `lua_load`.

Also as `lua_load`, this function only loads the chunk; it does not run it.

luaL_newlib

`void luaL_newlib (lua_State *L, const luaL_Reg l[]);` [-0, +1, m]

Creates a new table and registers there the functions in list l.

It is implemented as the following macro:

```
(luaL_newlibtable(L,l), luaL_setfuncs(L,l,0))
```

The array l must be the actual array, not a pointer to it.

luaL_newlibtable

`void luaL_newlibtable (lua_State *L, const luaL_Reg l[]);` [-0, +1, m]

Creates a new table with a size optimized to store all entries in the array l (but does not actually store them). It is intended to be used in conjunction with `luaL_setfuncs` (see `luaL_newlib`).

It is implemented as a macro. The array l must be the actual array, not a pointer to it.

luaL_newmetatable

`int luaL_newmetatable (lua_State *L, const char *tname);` [-0, +1, m]

If the registry already has the key tname, returns 0. Otherwise, creates a new table to be used as a metatable for userdata, adds to this new table the pair __name = tname, adds to the registry the pair [tname] = new table, and returns 1. (The entry __name is used by some error-reporting functions.)

In both cases pushes onto the stack the final value associated with tname in the registry.

luaL_newstate

`lua_State *luaL_newstate (void);` [-0, +0, –]

Creates a new Lua state. It calls `lua_newstate` with an allocator based on the standard C realloc function and then sets a panic function (see §4.6) that prints an error message to the standard error output in case of fatal errors.

Returns the new state, or NULL if there is a memory allocation error.

luaL_openlibs

`void luaL_openlibs (lua_State *L);` [-0, +0, e]

Opens all standard Lua libraries into the given state.

luaL_opt

```
T luaL_opt (L, func, arg, dflt);
```
[-0, +0, e]

This macro is defined as follows:

```
(lua_isnoneornil(L,(arg)) ? (dflt) : func(L,(arg)))
```

In words, if the argument arg is nil or absent, the macro results in the default dflt. Otherwise, it results in the result of calling func with the state L and the argument index arg as parameters. Note that it evaluates the expression dflt only if needed.

luaL_optinteger

```
lua_Integer luaL_optinteger (lua_State *L,
                             int arg,
                             lua_Integer d);
```
[-0, +0, v]

If the function argument arg is an integer (or convertible to an integer), returns this integer. If this argument is absent or is **nil**, returns d. Otherwise, raises an error.

luaL_optlstring

```
const char *luaL_optlstring (lua_State *L,
                             int arg,
                             const char *d,
                             size_t *l);
```
[-0, +0, v]

If the function argument arg is a string, returns this string. If this argument is absent or is **nil**, returns d. Otherwise, raises an error.

If l is not NULL, fills the position *l with the result's length. If the result is NULL (only possible when returning d and d == NULL), its length is considered zero.

luaL_optnumber

```
lua_Number luaL_optnumber (lua_State *L, int arg, lua_Number d);
```
[-0, +0, v]

If the function argument arg is a number, returns this number. If this argument is absent or is **nil**, returns d. Otherwise, raises an error.

luaL_optstring

```
const char *luaL_optstring (lua_State *L,
                            int arg,
                            const char *d);
```
[-0, +0, v]

If the function argument arg is a string, returns this string. If this argument is absent or is **nil**, returns d. Otherwise, raises an error.

luaL_prepbuffer

```
char *luaL_prepbuffer (luaL_Buffer *B);
```
[-?, +?, m]

Equivalent to luaL_prepbuffsize with the predefined size LUAL_BUFFERSIZE.

luaL_prepbuffsize

```
char *luaL_prepbuffsize (luaL_Buffer *B, size_t sz);
```
[-?, +?, *m*]

Returns an address to a space of size sz where you can copy a string to be added to buffer B (see luaL_Buffer). After copying the string into this space you must call luaL_addsize with the size of the string to actually add it to the buffer.

luaL_pushresult

```
void luaL_pushresult (luaL_Buffer *B);
```
[-?, +1, *m*]

Finishes the use of buffer B leaving the final string on the top of the stack.

luaL_pushresultsize

```
void luaL_pushresultsize (luaL_Buffer *B, size_t sz);
```
[-?, +1, *m*]

Equivalent to the sequence luaL_addsize, luaL_pushresult.

luaL_ref

```
int luaL_ref (lua_State *L, int t);
```
[-1, +0, *m*]

Creates and returns a *reference*, in the table at index t, for the object at the top of the stack (and pops the object).

A reference is a unique integer key. As long as you do not manually add integer keys into table t, luaL_ref ensures the uniqueness of the key it returns. You can retrieve an object referred by reference r by calling lua_rawgeti(L, t, r). Function luaL_unref frees a reference and its associated object.

If the object at the top of the stack is **nil**, luaL_ref returns the constant LUA_REFNIL. The constant LUA_NOREF is guaranteed to be different from any reference returned by luaL_ref.

luaL_Reg

```
typedef struct luaL_Reg {
  const char *name;
  lua_CFunction func;
} luaL_Reg;
```

Type for arrays of functions to be registered by luaL_setfuncs. name is the function name and func is a pointer to the function. Any array of luaL_Reg must end with a sentinel entry in which both name and func are NULL.

luaL_requiref

```
void luaL_requiref (lua_State *L, const char *modname,
                    lua_CFunction openf, int glb);
```
[-0, +1, *e*]

If modname is not already present in package.loaded, calls function openf with string modname as an argument and sets the call result in package.loaded[modname], as if that function has been called through require.

If glb is true, also stores the module into global modname.

Leaves a copy of the module on the stack.

luaL_setfuncs

```
void luaL_setfuncs (lua_State *L, const luaL_Reg *l, int nup);        [-nup, +0, m]
```

Registers all functions in the array l (see luaL_Reg) into the table on the top of the stack (below optional upvalues, see next).

When nup is not zero, all functions are created sharing nup upvalues, which must be previously pushed on the stack on top of the library table. These values are popped from the stack after the registration.

luaL_setmetatable

```
void luaL_setmetatable (lua_State *L, const char *tname);             [-0, +0, –]
```

Sets the metatable of the object at the top of the stack as the metatable associated with name tname in the registry (see luaL_newmetatable).

luaL_Stream

```
typedef struct luaL_Stream {
  FILE *f;
  lua_CFunction closef;
} luaL_Stream;
```

The standard representation for file handles, which is used by the standard I/O library.

A file handle is implemented as a full userdata, with a metatable called LUA_FILEHANDLE (where LUA_FILEHANDLE is a macro with the actual metatable's name). The metatable is created by the I/O library (see luaL_newmetatable).

This userdata must start with the structure luaL_Stream; it can contain other data after this initial structure. Field f points to the corresponding C stream (or it can be NULL to indicate an incompletely created handle). Field closef points to a Lua function that will be called to close the stream when the handle is closed or collected; this function receives the file handle as its sole argument and must return either **true** (in case of success) or **nil** plus an error message (in case of error). Once Lua calls this field, it changes the field value to NULL to signal that the handle is closed.

luaL_testudata

```
void *luaL_testudata (lua_State *L, int arg, const char *tname);      [-0, +0, m]
```

This function works like luaL_checkudata, except that, when the test fails, it returns NULL instead of raising an error.

luaL_tolstring

```
const char *luaL_tolstring (lua_State *L, int idx, size_t *len);      [-0, +1, e]
```

Converts any Lua value at the given index to a C string in a reasonable format. The resulting string is pushed onto the stack and also returned by the function. If len is not NULL, the function also sets *len with the string length.

If the value has a metatable with a __tostring field, then luaL_tolstring calls the corresponding metamethod with the value as argument, and uses the result of the call as its result.

luaL_traceback

```
void luaL_traceback (lua_State *L, lua_State *L1, const char *msg,        [-0, +1, m]
                     int level);
```

Creates and pushes a traceback of the stack L1. If msg is not NULL it is appended at the beginning of the traceback. The level parameter tells at which level to start the traceback.

luaL_typename

```
const char *luaL_typename (lua_State *L, int index);                     [-0, +0, –]
```

Returns the name of the type of the value at the given index.

luaL_unref

```
void luaL_unref (lua_State *L, int t, int ref);                          [-0, +0, –]
```

Releases reference ref from the table at index t (see luaL_ref). The entry is removed from the table, so that the referred object can be collected. The reference ref is also freed to be used again.

If ref is LUA_NOREF or LUA_REFNIL, luaL_unref does nothing.

luaL_where

```
void luaL_where (lua_State *L, int lvl);                                 [-0, +1, m]
```

Pushes onto the stack a string identifying the current position of the control at level lvl in the call stack. Typically this string has the following format:

> chunkname:currentline:

Level 0 is the running function, level 1 is the function that called the running function, etc.

This function is used to build a prefix for error messages.

6 – Standard Libraries

The standard Lua libraries provide useful functions that are implemented directly through the C API. Some of these functions provide essential services to the language (e.g., `type` and `getmetatable`); others provide access to "outside" services (e.g., I/O); and others could be implemented in Lua itself, but are quite useful or have critical performance requirements that deserve an implementation in C (e.g., `table.sort`).

All libraries are implemented through the official C API and are provided as separate C modules. Currently, Lua has the following standard libraries:

    basic library (§6.1);
    coroutine library (§6.2);
    package library (§6.3);
    string manipulation (§6.4);
    basic UTF-8 support (§6.5);
    table manipulation (§6.6);
    mathematical functions (§6.7) (sin, log, etc.);
    input and output (§6.8);
    operating system facilities (§6.9);
    debug facilities (§6.10).

Except for the basic and the package libraries, each library provides all its functions as fields of a global table or as methods of its objects.

To have access to these libraries, the C host program should call the `luaL_openlibs` function, which opens all standard libraries. Alternatively, the host program can open them individually by using `luaL_requiref` to call `luaopen_base` (for the basic library), `luaopen_package` (for the package library), `luaopen_coroutine` (for the coroutine library), `luaopen_string` (for the string library), `luaopen_utf8` (for the UTF8 library), `luaopen_table` (for the table library), `luaopen_math` (for the mathematical library), `luaopen_io` (for the I/O library), `luaopen_os` (for the operating system library), and `luaopen_debug` (for the debug library). These functions are declared in `lualib.h`.

6.1 – Basic Functions

The basic library provides core functions to Lua. If you do not include this library in your application, you should check carefully whether you need to provide implementations for some of its facilities.

assert (v [, message])

Calls `error` if the value of its argument v is false (i.e., **nil** or **false**); otherwise, returns all its arguments. In case of error, `message` is the error object; when absent, it defaults to "`assertion failed!`"

collectgarbage ([opt [, arg]])

This function is a generic interface to the garbage collector. It performs different functions according to its first argument, `opt`:

   "collect": performs a full garbage-collection cycle. This is the default option.
   "stop": stops automatic execution of the garbage collector. The collector will run only when explicitly invoked, until a call to restart it.
   "restart": restarts automatic execution of the garbage collector.

"count": returns the total memory in use by Lua in Kbytes. The value has a fractional part, so that it multiplied by 1024 gives the exact number of bytes in use by Lua (except for overflows).
"step": performs a garbage-collection step. The step "size" is controlled by arg. With a zero value, the collector will perform one basic (indivisible) step. For non-zero values, the collector will perform as if that amount of memory (in KBytes) had been allocated by Lua. Returns **true** if the step finished a collection cycle.
"setpause": sets arg as the new value for the *pause* of the collector (see §2.5). Returns the previous value for *pause*.
"setstepmul": sets arg as the new value for the *step multiplier* of the collector (see §2.5). Returns the previous value for *step*.
"isrunning": returns a boolean that tells whether the collector is running (i.e., not stopped).

dofile ([filename])

Opens the named file and executes its contents as a Lua chunk. When called without arguments, dofile executes the contents of the standard input (stdin). Returns all values returned by the chunk. In case of errors, dofile propagates the error to its caller (that is, dofile does not run in protected mode).

error (message [, level])

Terminates the last protected function called and returns message as the error object. Function error never returns.

Usually, error adds some information about the error position at the beginning of the message, if the message is a string. The level argument specifies how to get the error position. With level 1 (the default), the error position is where the error function was called. Level 2 points the error to where the function that called error was called; and so on. Passing a level 0 avoids the addition of error position information to the message.

_G

A global variable (not a function) that holds the global environment (see §2.2). Lua itself does not use this variable; changing its value does not affect any environment, nor vice versa.

getmetatable (object)

If object does not have a metatable, returns **nil**. Otherwise, if the object's metatable has a __metatable field, returns the associated value. Otherwise, returns the metatable of the given object.

ipairs (t)

Returns three values (an iterator function, the table t, and 0) so that the construction

```
for i,v in ipairs(t) do body end
```

will iterate over the key–value pairs (1,t[1]), (2,t[2]), ..., up to the first nil value.

load (chunk [, chunkname [, mode [, env]]])

Loads a chunk.

If chunk is a string, the chunk is this string. If chunk is a function, load calls it repeatedly to get the chunk pieces. Each call to chunk must return a string that concatenates with previous results. A return of an empty string, **nil**, or no value signals the end of the chunk.

If there are no syntactic errors, returns the compiled chunk as a function; otherwise, returns **nil** plus the error message.

If the resulting function has upvalues, the first upvalue is set to the value of env, if that parameter is given, or to the value of the global environment. Other upvalues are initialized with **nil**. (When you load a main chunk, the resulting function will always have exactly one upvalue, the _ENV variable (see §2.2). However, when you load a binary chunk created from a function (see `string.dump`), the resulting function can have an arbitrary number of upvalues.) All upvalues are fresh, that is, they are not shared with any other function.

`chunkname` is used as the name of the chunk for error messages and debug information (see §4.9). When absent, it defaults to `chunk`, if `chunk` is a string, or to `"=(load)"` otherwise.

The string `mode` controls whether the chunk can be text or binary (that is, a precompiled chunk). It may be the string `"b"` (only binary chunks), `"t"` (only text chunks), or `"bt"` (both binary and text). The default is `"bt"`.

Lua does not check the consistency of binary chunks. Maliciously crafted binary chunks can crash the interpreter.

loadfile ([filename [, mode [, env]]])

Similar to `load`, but gets the chunk from file `filename` or from the standard input, if no file name is given.

next (table [, index])

Allows a program to traverse all fields of a table. Its first argument is a table and its second argument is an index in this table. `next` returns the next index of the table and its associated value. When called with **nil** as its second argument, `next` returns an initial index and its associated value. When called with the last index, or with **nil** in an empty table, `next` returns **nil**. If the second argument is absent, then it is interpreted as **nil**. In particular, you can use `next(t)` to check whether a table is empty.

The order in which the indices are enumerated is not specified, *even for numeric indices*. (To traverse a table in numerical order, use a numerical **for**.)

The behavior of `next` is undefined if, during the traversal, you assign any value to a non-existent field in the table. You may however modify existing fields. In particular, you may clear existing fields.

pairs (t)

If t has a metamethod __pairs, calls it with t as argument and returns the first three results from the call.

Otherwise, returns three values: the `next` function, the table t, and **nil**, so that the construction

        for k,v in pairs(t) do *body* end

will iterate over all key–value pairs of table t.

See function `next` for the caveats of modifying the table during its traversal.

pcall (f [, arg1, ⋯])

Calls function f with the given arguments in *protected mode*. This means that any error inside f is not propagated; instead, pcall catches the error and returns a status code. Its first result is the status code (a boolean), which is true if the call succeeds without errors. In such case, pcall also returns all results from the call, after this first result. In case of any error, `pcall` returns **false** plus the error message.

print (···)

Receives any number of arguments and prints their values to `stdout`, using the `tostring` function to convert each argument to a string. `print` is not intended for formatted output, but only as a quick way to show a value, for instance for debugging. For complete control over the output, use `string.format` and `io.write`.

rawequal (v1, v2)

Checks whether v1 is equal to v2, without invoking the __eq metamethod. Returns a boolean.

rawget (table, index)

Gets the real value of `table[index]`, without invoking the __index metamethod. `table` must be a table; `index` may be any value.

rawlen (v)

Returns the length of the object v, which must be a table or a string, without invoking the __len metamethod. Returns an integer.

rawset (table, index, value)

Sets the real value of `table[index]` to `value`, without invoking the __newindex metamethod. `table` must be a table, `index` any value different from **nil** and NaN, and `value` any Lua value.

This function returns `table`.

select (index, ···)

If `index` is a number, returns all arguments after argument number `index`; a negative number indexes from the end (-1 is the last argument). Otherwise, `index` must be the string "#", and `select` returns the total number of extra arguments it received.

setmetatable (table, metatable)

Sets the metatable for the given table. (To change the metatable of other types from Lua code, you must use the debug library (§6.10).) If `metatable` is **nil**, removes the metatable of the given table. If the original metatable has a __metatable field, raises an error.

This function returns `table`.

tonumber (e [, base])

When called with no `base`, `tonumber` tries to convert its argument to a number. If the argument is already a number or a string convertible to a number, then `tonumber` returns this number; otherwise, it returns **nil**.

The conversion of strings can result in integers or floats, according to the lexical conventions of Lua (see §3.1). (The string may have leading and trailing spaces and a sign.)

When called with `base`, then e must be a string to be interpreted as an integer numeral in that base. The base may be any integer between 2 and 36, inclusive. In bases above 10, the letter 'A' (in either upper or lower case) represents 10, 'B' represents 11, and so forth, with 'Z' representing 35. If the string e is not a valid numeral in the given base, the function returns **nil**.

tostring (v)

Receives a value of any type and converts it to a string in a human-readable format. (For complete control of how numbers are converted, use `string.format`.)

If the metatable of v has a __tostring field, then `tostring` calls the corresponding value with v as argument, and uses the result of the call as its result.

type (v)

Returns the type of its only argument, coded as a string. The possible results of this function are "nil" (a string, not the value **nil**), "number", "string", "boolean", "table", "function", "thread", and "userdata".

_VERSION

A global variable (not a function) that holds a string containing the running Lua version. The current value of this variable is "Lua 5.3".

xpcall (f, msgh [, arg1, ···])

This function is similar to `pcall`, except that it sets a new message handler `msgh`.

6.2 – Coroutine Manipulation

This library comprises the operations to manipulate coroutines, which come inside the table `coroutine`. See §2.6 for a general description of coroutines.

coroutine.create (f)

Creates a new coroutine, with body f. f must be a function. Returns this new coroutine, an object with type "thread".

coroutine.isyieldable ()

Returns true when the running coroutine can yield.

A running coroutine is yieldable if it is not the main thread and it is not inside a non-yieldable C function.

coroutine.resume (co [, val1, ···])

Starts or continues the execution of coroutine co. The first time you resume a coroutine, it starts running its body. The values val1, ... are passed as the arguments to the body function. If the coroutine has yielded, `resume` restarts it; the values val1, ... are passed as the results from the yield.

If the coroutine runs without any errors, `resume` returns **true** plus any values passed to `yield` (when the coroutine yields) or any values returned by the body function (when the coroutine terminates). If there is any error, `resume` returns **false** plus the error message.

coroutine.running ()

Returns the running coroutine plus a boolean, true when the running coroutine is the main one.

coroutine.status (co)

Returns the status of coroutine `co`, as a string: `"running"`, if the coroutine is running (that is, it called `status`); `"suspended"`, if the coroutine is suspended in a call to `yield`, or if it has not started running yet; `"normal"` if the coroutine is active but not running (that is, it has resumed another coroutine); and `"dead"` if the coroutine has finished its body function, or if it has stopped with an error.

coroutine.wrap (f)

Creates a new coroutine, with body `f`. `f` must be a function. Returns a function that resumes the coroutine each time it is called. Any arguments passed to the function behave as the extra arguments to `resume`. Returns the same values returned by `resume`, except the first boolean. In case of error, propagates the error.

coroutine.yield (···)

Suspends the execution of the calling coroutine. Any arguments to `yield` are passed as extra results to `resume`.

6.3 – Modules

The package library provides basic facilities for loading modules in Lua. It exports one function directly in the global environment: `require`. Everything else is exported in a table `package`.

require (modname)

Loads the given module. The function starts by looking into the `package.loaded` table to determine whether `modname` is already loaded. If it is, then `require` returns the value stored at `package.loaded[modname]`. Otherwise, it tries to find a *loader* for the module.

To find a loader, `require` is guided by the `package.searchers` sequence. By changing this sequence, we can change how `require` looks for a module. The following explanation is based on the default configuration for `package.searchers`.

First `require` queries `package.preload[modname]`. If it has a value, this value (which must be a function) is the loader. Otherwise `require` searches for a Lua loader using the path stored in `package.path`. If that also fails, it searches for a C loader using the path stored in `package.cpath`. If that also fails, it tries an *all-in-one* loader (see `package.searchers`).

Once a loader is found, `require` calls the loader with two arguments: `modname` and an extra value dependent on how it got the loader. (If the loader came from a file, this extra value is the file name.) If the loader returns any non-nil value, `require` assigns the returned value to `package.loaded[modname]`. If the loader does not return a non-nil value and has not assigned any value to `package.loaded[modname]`, then `require` assigns **true** to this entry. In any case, `require` returns the final value of `package.loaded[modname]`.

If there is any error loading or running the module, or if it cannot find any loader for the module, then `require` raises an error.

package.config

A string describing some compile-time configurations for packages. This string is a sequence of lines:

The first line is the directory separator string. Default is '\' for Windows and '/' for all other systems.

The second line is the character that separates templates in a path. Default is ';'.

The third line is the string that marks the substitution points in a template. Default is '?'.

The fourth line is a string that, in a path in Windows, is replaced by the executable's directory. Default is '!'.

The fifth line is a mark to ignore all text after it when building the luaopen_ function name. Default is '-'.

package.cpath

The path used by require to search for a C loader.

Lua initializes the C path package.cpath in the same way it initializes the Lua path package.path, using the environment variable LUA_CPATH_5_3 or the environment variable LUA_CPATH or a default path defined in luaconf.h.

package.loaded

A table used by require to control which modules are already loaded. When you require a module modname and package.loaded[modname] is not false, require simply returns the value stored there.

This variable is only a reference to the real table; assignments to this variable do not change the table used by require.

package.loadlib (libname, funcname)

Dynamically links the host program with the C library libname.

If funcname is "*", then it only links with the library, making the symbols exported by the library available to other dynamically linked libraries. Otherwise, it looks for a function funcname inside the library and returns this function as a C function. So, funcname must follow the lua_CFunction prototype (see lua_CFunction).

This is a low-level function. It completely bypasses the package and module system. Unlike require, it does not perform any path searching and does not automatically adds extensions. libname must be the complete file name of the C library, including if necessary a path and an extension. funcname must be the exact name exported by the C library (which may depend on the C compiler and linker used).

This function is not supported by Standard C. As such, it is only available on some platforms (Windows, Linux, Mac OS X, Solaris, BSD, plus other Unix systems that support the dlfcn standard).

package.path

The path used by require to search for a Lua loader.

At start-up, Lua initializes this variable with the value of the environment variable LUA_PATH_5_3 or the environment variable LUA_PATH or with a default path defined in luaconf.h, if those environment variables are not defined. Any ";;" in the value of the environment variable is replaced by the default path.

package.preload

A table to store loaders for specific modules (see require).

This variable is only a reference to the real table; assignments to this variable do not change the table used by require.

package.searchers

A table used by `require` to control how to load modules.

Each entry in this table is a *searcher function*. When looking for a module, `require` calls each of these searchers in ascending order, with the module name (the argument given to `require`) as its sole parameter. The function can return another function (the module *loader*) plus an extra value that will be passed to that loader, or a string explaining why it did not find that module (or **nil** if it has nothing to say).

Lua initializes this table with four searcher functions.

The first searcher simply looks for a loader in the `package.preload` table.

The second searcher looks for a loader as a Lua library, using the path stored at `package.path`. The search is done as described in function `package.searchpath`.

The third searcher looks for a loader as a C library, using the path given by the variable `package.cpath`. Again, the search is done as described in function `package.searchpath`. For instance, if the C path is the string

        "./?.so;./?.dll;/usr/local/?/init.so"

the searcher for module `foo` will try to open the files `./foo.so`, `./foo.dll`, and `/usr/local/foo/init.so`, in that order. Once it finds a C library, this searcher first uses a dynamic link facility to link the application with the library. Then it tries to find a C function inside the library to be used as the loader. The name of this C function is the string `"luaopen_"` concatenated with a copy of the module name where each dot is replaced by an underscore. Moreover, if the module name has a hyphen, its suffix after (and including) the first hyphen is removed. For instance, if the module name is `a.b.c-v2.1`, the function name will be `luaopen_a_b_c`.

The fourth searcher tries an *all-in-one loader*. It searches the C path for a library for the root name of the given module. For instance, when requiring `a.b.c`, it will search for a C library for `a`. If found, it looks into it for an open function for the submodule; in our example, that would be `luaopen_a_b_c`. With this facility, a package can pack several C submodules into one single library, with each submodule keeping its original open function.

All searchers except the first one (preload) return as the extra value the file name where the module was found, as returned by `package.searchpath`. The first searcher returns no extra value.

package.searchpath (name, path [, sep [, rep]])

Searches for the given `name` in the given `path`.

A path is a string containing a sequence of *templates* separated by semicolons. For each template, the function replaces each interrogation mark (if any) in the template with a copy of name wherein all occurrences of sep (a dot, by default) were replaced by rep (the system's directory separator, by default), and then tries to open the resulting file name.

For instance, if the path is the string

        "./?.lua;./?.lc;/usr/local/?/init.lua"

the search for the name `foo.a` will try to open the files `./foo/a.lua`, `./foo/a.lc`, and `/usr/local/foo/a/init.lua`, in that order.

Returns the resulting name of the first file that it can open in read mode (after closing the file), or **nil** plus an error message if none succeeds. (This error message lists all file names it tried to open.)

6.4 – String Manipulation

This library provides generic functions for string manipulation, such as finding and extracting substrings, and pattern matching. When indexing a string in Lua, the first character is at position 1 (not at 0, as in C). Indices are allowed to be negative and are interpreted as indexing backwards, from the end of the string. Thus, the last character is at position -1, and so on.

The string library provides all its functions inside the table `string`. It also sets a metatable for strings where the `__index` field points to the `string` table. Therefore, you can use the string functions in object-oriented style. For instance, `string.byte(s,i)` can be written as `s:byte(i)`.

The string library assumes one-byte character encodings.

string.byte (s [, i [, j]])

Returns the internal numeric codes of the characters `s[i]`, `s[i+1]`, ..., `s[j]`. The default value for i is 1; the default value for j is i. These indices are corrected following the same rules of function `string.sub`.

Numeric codes are not necessarily portable across platforms.

string.char (···)

Receives zero or more integers. Returns a string with length equal to the number of arguments, in which each character has the internal numeric code equal to its corresponding argument.

Numeric codes are not necessarily portable across platforms.

string.dump (function [, strip])

Returns a string containing a binary representation (a *binary chunk*) of the given function, so that a later `load` on this string returns a copy of the function (but with new upvalues). If `strip` is a true value, the binary representation may not include all debug information about the function, to save space.

Functions with upvalues have only their number of upvalues saved. When (re)loaded, those upvalues receive fresh instances containing **nil**. (You can use the debug library to serialize and reload the upvalues of a function in a way adequate to your needs.)

string.find (s, pattern [, init [, plain]])

Looks for the first match of `pattern` (see §6.4.1) in the string s. If it finds a match, then `find` returns the indices of s where this occurrence starts and ends; otherwise, it returns **nil**. A third, optional numeric argument `init` specifies where to start the search; its default value is 1 and can be negative. A value of **true** as a fourth, optional argument `plain` turns off the pattern matching facilities, so the function does a plain "find substring" operation, with no characters in `pattern` being considered magic. Note that if `plain` is given, then `init` must be given as well.

If the pattern has captures, then in a successful match the captured values are also returned, after the two indices.

string.format (formatstring, ···)

Returns a formatted version of its variable number of arguments following the description given in its first argument (which must be a string). The format string follows the same rules as the ISO C function `sprintf`. The only differences are that the options/modifiers *, h, L, l, n, and p are not supported and that there is an extra option, q.

The q option formats a string between double quotes, using escape sequences when necessary to ensure that it can safely be read back by the Lua interpreter. For instance, the call

```
string.format('%q', 'a string with "quotes" and \n new line')
```

may produce the string:

```
"a string with \"quotes\" and \
new line"
```

Options A, a, E, e, f, G, and g all expect a number as argument. Options c, d, i, o, u, X, and x expect an integer. When Lua is compiled with a C89 compiler, options A and a (hexadecimal floats) do not support any modifier (flags, width, length).

Option s expects a string; if its argument is not a string, it is converted to one following the same rules of tostring. If the option has any modifier (flags, width, length), the string argument should not contain embedded zeros.

string.gmatch (s, pattern)

Returns an iterator function that, each time it is called, returns the next captures from pattern (see §6.4.1) over the string s. If pattern specifies no captures, then the whole match is produced in each call.

As an example, the following loop will iterate over all the words from string s, printing one per line:

```
s = "hello world from Lua"
for w in string.gmatch(s, "%a+") do
  print(w)
end
```

The next example collects all pairs key=value from the given string into a table:

```
t = {}
s = "from=world, to=Lua"
for k, v in string.gmatch(s, "(%w+)=(%w+)") do
  t[k] = v
end
```

For this function, a caret '^' at the start of a pattern does not work as an anchor, as this would prevent the iteration.

string.gsub (s, pattern, repl [, n])

Returns a copy of s in which all (or the first n, if given) occurrences of the pattern (see §6.4.1) have been replaced by a replacement string specified by repl, which can be a string, a table, or a function. gsub also returns, as its second value, the total number of matches that occurred. The name gsub comes from *Global SUBstitution*.

If repl is a string, then its value is used for replacement. The character % works as an escape character: any sequence in repl of the form %*d*, with *d* between 1 and 9, stands for the value of the *d*-th captured substring. The sequence %0 stands for the whole match. The sequence %% stands for a single %.

If repl is a table, then the table is queried for every match, using the first capture as the key.

If repl is a function, then this function is called every time a match occurs, with all captured substrings passed as arguments, in order.

In any case, if the pattern specifies no captures, then it behaves as if the whole pattern was inside a capture.

If the value returned by the table query or by the function call is a string or a number, then it is used as the replacement string; otherwise, if it is **false** or **nil**, then there is no replacement (that is, the original match is kept in the string).

Here are some examples:

```
x = string.gsub("hello world", "(%w+)", "%1 %1")
--> x="hello hello world world"

x = string.gsub("hello world", "%w+", "%0 %0", 1)
--> x="hello hello world"

x = string.gsub("hello world from Lua", "(%w+)%s*(%w+)", "%2 %1")
--> x="world hello Lua from"

x = string.gsub("home = $HOME, user = $USER", "%$(%w+)", os.getenv)
--> x="home = /home/roberto, user = roberto"

x = string.gsub("4+5 = $return 4+5$", "%$(.-)%$", function (s)
      return load(s)()
    end)
--> x="4+5 = 9"

local t = {name="lua", version="5.3"}
x = string.gsub("$name-$version.tar.gz", "%$(%w+)", t)
--> x="lua-5.3.tar.gz"
```

string.len (s)

Receives a string and returns its length. The empty string "" has length 0. Embedded zeros are counted, so "a\000bc\000" has length 5.

string.lower (s)

Receives a string and returns a copy of this string with all uppercase letters changed to lowercase. All other characters are left unchanged. The definition of what an uppercase letter is depends on the current locale.

string.match (s, pattern [, init])

Looks for the first *match* of pattern (see §6.4.1) in the string s. If it finds one, then match returns the captures from the pattern; otherwise it returns **nil**. If pattern specifies no captures, then the whole match is returned. A third, optional numeric argument init specifies where to start the search; its default value is 1 and can be negative.

string.pack (fmt, v1, v2, ···)

Returns a binary string containing the values v1, v2, etc. packed (that is, serialized in binary form) according to the format string fmt (see §6.4.2).

string.packsize (fmt)

Returns the size of a string resulting from string.pack with the given format. The format string cannot have the variable-length options 's' or 'z' (see §6.4.2).

string.rep (s, n [, sep])

Returns a string that is the concatenation of n copies of the string s separated by the string sep. The default value for sep is the empty string (that is, no separator). Returns the empty string if n is not positive.

(Note that it is very easy to exhaust the memory of your machine with a single call to this function.)

string.reverse (s)

Returns a string that is the string s reversed.

string.sub (s, i [, j])

Returns the substring of s that starts at i and continues until j; i and j can be negative. If j is absent, then it is assumed to be equal to -1 (which is the same as the string length). In particular, the call string.sub(s,1,j) returns a prefix of s with length j, and string.sub(s, -i) returns a suffix of s with length i.

If, after the translation of negative indices, i is less than 1, it is corrected to 1. If j is greater than the string length, it is corrected to that length. If, after these corrections, i is greater than j, the function returns the empty string.

string.unpack (fmt, s [, pos])

Returns the values packed in string s (see string.pack) according to the format string fmt (see §6.4.2). An optional pos marks where to start reading in s (default is 1). After the read values, this function also returns the index of the first unread byte in s.

string.upper (s)

Receives a string and returns a copy of this string with all lowercase letters changed to uppercase. All other characters are left unchanged. The definition of what a lowercase letter is depends on the current locale.

6.4.1 – Patterns

Patterns in Lua are described by regular strings, which are interpreted as patterns by the pattern-matching functions string.find, string.gmatch, string.gsub, and string.match. This section describes the syntax and the meaning (that is, what they match) of these strings.

Character Class:

A *character class* is used to represent a set of characters. The following combinations are allowed in describing a character class:

> **x:** (where *x* is not one of the *magic characters* ^$()%.[]*+-?) represents the character *x* itself.
> **.:** (a dot) represents all characters.
> **%a:** represents all letters.
> **%c:** represents all control characters.
> **%d:** represents all digits.
> **%g:** represents all printable characters except space.
> **%l:** represents all lowercase letters.
> **%p:** represents all punctuation characters.
> **%s:** represents all space characters.
> **%u:** represents all uppercase letters.

%w: represents all alphanumeric characters.

%x: represents all hexadecimal digits.

%*x*: (where *x* is any non-alphanumeric character) represents the character *x*. This is the standard way to escape the magic characters. Any non-alphanumeric character (including all punctuation characters, even the non-magical) can be preceded by a '%' when used to represent itself in a pattern.

[*set*]: represents the class which is the union of all characters in *set*. A range of characters can be specified by separating the end characters of the range, in ascending order, with a '-'. All classes %x described above can also be used as components in *set*. All other characters in *set* represent themselves. For example, [%w_] (or [_%w]) represents all alphanumeric characters plus the underscore, [0-7] represents the octal digits, and [0-7%l%-] represents the octal digits plus the lowercase letters plus the '-' character.

You can put a closing square bracket in a set by positioning it as the first character in the set. You can put an hyphen in a set by positioning it as the first or the last character in the set. (You can also use an escape for both cases.)

The interaction between ranges and classes is not defined. Therefore, patterns like [%a-z] or [a-%%] have no meaning.

[^*set*]: represents the complement of *set*, where *set* is interpreted as above.

For all classes represented by single letters (%a, %c, etc.), the corresponding uppercase letter represents the complement of the class. For instance, %S represents all non-space characters.

The definitions of letter, space, and other character groups depend on the current locale. In particular, the class [a-z] may not be equivalent to %l.

Pattern Item:

A *pattern item* can be

  a single character class, which matches any single character in the class;
  a single character class followed by '*', which matches zero or more repetitions of characters in the class. These repetition items will always match the longest possible sequence;
  a single character class followed by '+', which matches one or more repetitions of characters in the class. These repetition items will always match the longest possible sequence;
  a single character class followed by '-', which also matches zero or more repetitions of characters in the class. Unlike '*', these repetition items will always match the shortest possible sequence;
  a single character class followed by '?', which matches zero or one occurrence of a character in the class. It always matches one occurrence if possible;
  %*n*, for *n* between 1 and 9; such item matches a substring equal to the *n*-th captured string (see below);
  %b*xy*, where *x* and *y* are two distinct characters; such item matches strings that start with *x*, end with *y*, and where the *x* and *y* are *balanced*. This means that, if one reads the string from left to right, counting +1 for an *x* and -1 for a *y*, the ending *y* is the first *y* where the count reaches 0. For instance, the item %b() matches expressions with balanced parentheses.
  %f[*set*], a *frontier pattern*; such item matches an empty string at any position such that the next character belongs to *set* and the previous character does not belong to *set*. The set *set* is interpreted as previously described. The beginning and the end of the subject are handled as if they were the character '\0'.

Pattern:

A *pattern* is a sequence of pattern items. A caret '^' at the beginning of a pattern anchors the match at the beginning of the subject string. A '$' at the end of a pattern anchors the match at the end of the subject string. At other positions, '^' and '$' have no special meaning and represent themselves.

Captures:

A pattern can contain sub-patterns enclosed in parentheses; they describe *captures*. When a match succeeds, the substrings of the subject string that match captures are stored (*captured*) for future use. Captures are numbered according to their left parentheses. For instance, in the pattern "(a* (.)%w(%s*))", the part of the string matching "a*(.)%w(%s*)" is stored as the first capture (and therefore has number 1); the character matching "." is captured with number 2, and the part matching "%s*" has number 3.

As a special case, the empty capture () captures the current string position (a number). For instance, if we apply the pattern "()aa()" on the string "flaaap", there will be two captures: 3 and 5.

6.4.2 – Format Strings for Pack and Unpack

The first argument to `string.pack`, `string.packsize`, and `string.unpack` is a format string, which describes the layout of the structure being created or read.

A format string is a sequence of conversion options. The conversion options are as follows:

> **<**: sets little endian
> **>**: sets big endian
> **=**: sets native endian
> **![*n*]**: sets maximum alignment to n (default is native alignment)
> **b**: a signed byte (`char`)
> **B**: an unsigned byte (`char`)
> **h**: a signed `short` (native size)
> **H**: an unsigned `short` (native size)
> **l**: a signed `long` (native size)
> **L**: an unsigned `long` (native size)
> **j**: a `lua_Integer`
> **J**: a `lua_Unsigned`
> **T**: a `size_t` (native size)
> **i[*n*]**: a signed `int` with n bytes (default is native size)
> **I[*n*]**: an unsigned `int` with n bytes (default is native size)
> **f**: a `float` (native size)
> **d**: a `double` (native size)
> **n**: a `lua_Number`
> **c*n***: a fixed-sized string with n bytes
> **z**: a zero-terminated string
> **s[*n*]**: a string preceded by its length coded as an unsigned integer with n bytes (default is a `size_t`)
> **x**: one byte of padding
> **X*op***: an empty item that aligns according to option op (which is otherwise ignored)
> **' '**: (empty space) ignored

(A "[*n*]" means an optional integral numeral.) Except for padding, spaces, and configurations (options "xX <=>!"), each option corresponds to an argument (in `string.pack`) or a result (in `string.unpack`).

For options "!*n*", "s*n*", "i*n*", and "I*n*", n can be any integer between 1 and 16. All integral options check overflows; `string.pack` checks whether the given value fits in the given size; `string.unpack` checks whether the read value fits in a Lua integer.

Any format string starts as if prefixed by "!1=", that is, with maximum alignment of 1 (no alignment) and native endianness.

Alignment works as follows: For each option, the format gets extra padding until the data starts at an offset that is a multiple of the minimum between the option size and the maximum alignment; this minimum must be a power of 2. Options "c" and "z" are not aligned; option "s" follows the alignment of its starting integer.

All padding is filled with zeros by `string.pack` (and ignored by `string.unpack`).

6.5 – UTF-8 Support

This library provides basic support for UTF-8 encoding. It provides all its functions inside the table `utf8`. This library does not provide any support for Unicode other than the handling of the encoding. Any operation that needs the meaning of a character, such as character classification, is outside its scope.

Unless stated otherwise, all functions that expect a byte position as a parameter assume that the given position is either the start of a byte sequence or one plus the length of the subject string. As in the string library, negative indices count from the end of the string.

utf8.char (···)

Receives zero or more integers, converts each one to its corresponding UTF-8 byte sequence and returns a string with the concatenation of all these sequences.

utf8.charpattern

The pattern (a string, not a function) "[\0-\x7F\xC2-\xF4][\x80-\xBF]*" (see §6.4.1), which matches exactly one UTF-8 byte sequence, assuming that the subject is a valid UTF-8 string.

utf8.codes (s)

Returns values so that the construction

```
for p, c in utf8.codes(s) do body end
```

will iterate over all characters in string s, with p being the position (in bytes) and c the code point of each character. It raises an error if it meets any invalid byte sequence.

utf8.codepoint (s [, i [, j]])

Returns the codepoints (as integers) from all characters in s that start between byte position i and j (both included). The default for i is 1 and for j is i. It raises an error if it meets any invalid byte sequence.

utf8.len (s [, i [, j]])

Returns the number of UTF-8 characters in string s that start between positions i and j (both inclusive). The default for i is 1 and for j is -1. If it finds any invalid byte sequence, returns a false value plus the position of the first invalid byte.

utf8.offset (s, n [, i])

Returns the position (in bytes) where the encoding of the n-th character of s (counting from position i) starts. A negative n gets characters before position i. The default for i is 1 when n is non-negative and #s + 1 otherwise, so that `utf8.offset(s, -n)` gets the offset of the n-th character from the end of the string. If the specified character is neither in the subject nor right after its end, the function returns **nil**.

As a special case, when n is 0 the function returns the start of the encoding of the character that contains the i-th byte of s.

This function assumes that s is a valid UTF-8 string.

6.6 – Table Manipulation

This library provides generic functions for table manipulation. It provides all its functions inside the table `table`.

Remember that, whenever an operation needs the length of a table, the table must be a proper sequence or have a __len metamethod (see §3.4.7). All functions ignore non-numeric keys in the tables given as arguments.

table.concat (list [, sep [, i [, j]]])

Given a list where all elements are strings or numbers, returns the string `list[i]..sep..list[i+1] ··· sep..list[j]`. The default value for sep is the empty string, the default for i is 1, and the default for j is #list. If i is greater than j, returns the empty string.

table.insert (list, [pos,] value)

Inserts element value at position pos in list, shifting up the elements `list[pos]`, `list[pos+1]`, ···, `list[#list]`. The default value for pos is #list+1, so that a call `table.insert(t,x)` inserts x at the end of list t.

table.move (a1, f, e, t [,a2])

Moves elements from table a1 to table a2, performing the equivalent to the following multiple assignment: `a2[t],··· = a1[f],···,a1[e]`. The default for a2 is a1. The destination range can overlap with the source range. The number of elements to be moved must fit in a Lua integer.

Returns the destination table a2.

table.pack (···)

Returns a new table with all parameters stored into keys 1, 2, etc. and with a field "n" with the total number of parameters. Note that the resulting table may not be a sequence.

table.remove (list [, pos])

Removes from `list` the element at position pos, returning the value of the removed element. When pos is an integer between 1 and #list, it shifts down the elements `list[pos+1]`, `list[pos+2]`, ···, `list[#list]` and erases element `list[#list]`; The index pos can also be 0 when #list is 0, or #list + 1; in those cases, the function erases the element `list[pos]`.

The default value for pos is #list, so that a call `table.remove(l)` removes the last element of list l.

table.sort (list [, comp])

Sorts list elements in a given order, *in-place*, from `list[1]` to `list[#list]`. If comp is given, then it must be a function that receives two list elements and returns true when the first element must come before the second in the final order (so that, after the sort, i < j implies not `comp(list[j],list[i])`). If comp is not given, then the standard Lua operator < is used instead.

Note that the `comp` function must define a strict partial order over the elements in the list; that is, it must be asymmetric and transitive. Otherwise, no valid sort may be possible.

The sort algorithm is not stable; that is, elements not comparable by the given order (e.g., equal elements) may have their relative positions changed by the sort.

table.unpack (list [, i [, j]])

Returns the elements from the given list. This function is equivalent to

```
return list[i], list[i+1], ···, list[j]
```

By default, i is 1 and j is #list.

6.7 – Mathematical Functions

This library provides basic mathematical functions. It provides all its functions and constants inside the table `math`. Functions with the annotation `"integer/float"` give integer results for integer arguments and float results for float (or mixed) arguments. Rounding functions (`math.ceil`, `math.floor`, and `math.modf`) return an integer when the result fits in the range of an integer, or a float otherwise.

math.abs (x)

Returns the absolute value of x. (integer/float)

math.acos (x)

Returns the arc cosine of x (in radians).

math.asin (x)

Returns the arc sine of x (in radians).

math.atan (y [, x])

Returns the arc tangent of y/x (in radians), but uses the signs of both parameters to find the quadrant of the result. (It also handles correctly the case of x being zero.)

The default value for x is 1, so that the call `math.atan(y)` returns the arc tangent of y.

math.ceil (x)

Returns the smallest integral value larger than or equal to x.

math.cos (x)

Returns the cosine of x (assumed to be in radians).

math.deg (x)

Converts the angle x from radians to degrees.

math.exp (x)

Returns the value e^x (where e is the base of natural logarithms).

math.floor (x)

Returns the largest integral value smaller than or equal to x.

math.fmod (x, y)

Returns the remainder of the division of x by y that rounds the quotient towards zero. (integer/float)

math.huge

The float value HUGE_VAL, a value larger than any other numeric value.

math.log (x [, base])

Returns the logarithm of x in the given base. The default for base is e (so that the function returns the natural logarithm of x).

math.max (x, ···)

Returns the argument with the maximum value, according to the Lua operator <. (integer/float)

math.maxinteger

An integer with the maximum value for an integer.

math.min (x, ···)

Returns the argument with the minimum value, according to the Lua operator <. (integer/float)

math.mininteger

An integer with the minimum value for an integer.

math.modf (x)

Returns the integral part of x and the fractional part of x. Its second result is always a float.

math.pi

The value of π.

math.rad (x)

Converts the angle x from degrees to radians.

math.random ([m [, n]])

When called without arguments, returns a pseudo-random float with uniform distribution in the range [0,1). When called with two integers m and n, math.random returns a pseudo-random integer with uniform distribution in the range [m, n]. (The value n-m cannot be negative and must fit in a Lua integer.) The call math.random(n) is equivalent to math.random(1,n).

This function is an interface to the underling pseudo-random generator function provided by C.

math.randomseed (x)

Sets x as the "seed" for the pseudo-random generator: equal seeds produce equal sequences of numbers.

math.sin (x)

Returns the sine of x (assumed to be in radians).

math.sqrt (x)

Returns the square root of x. (You can also use the expression x^0.5 to compute this value.)

math.tan (x)

Returns the tangent of x (assumed to be in radians).

math.tointeger (x)

If the value x is convertible to an integer, returns that integer. Otherwise, returns **nil**.

math.type (x)

Returns "integer" if x is an integer, "float" if it is a float, or **nil** if x is not a number.

math.ult (m, n)

Returns a boolean, true if integer m is below integer n when they are compared as unsigned integers.

6.8 – Input and Output Facilities

The I/O library provides two different styles for file manipulation. The first one uses implicit file handles; that is, there are operations to set a default input file and a default output file, and all input/output operations are over these default files. The second style uses explicit file handles.

When using implicit file handles, all operations are supplied by table io. When using explicit file handles, the operation io.open returns a file handle and then all operations are supplied as methods of the file handle.

The table io also provides three predefined file handles with their usual meanings from C: io.stdin, io.stdout, and io.stderr. The I/O library never closes these files.

Unless otherwise stated, all I/O functions return **nil** on failure (plus an error message as a second result and a system-dependent error code as a third result) and some value different from **nil** on success. On non-POSIX systems, the computation of the error message and error code in case of errors may be not thread safe, because they rely on the global C variable errno.

io.close ([file])

Equivalent to file:close(). Without a file, closes the default output file.

io.flush ()

Equivalent to io.output():flush().

io.input ([file])

When called with a file name, it opens the named file (in text mode), and sets its handle as the default input file. When called with a file handle, it simply sets this file handle as the default input file. When called without parameters, it returns the current default input file.

In case of errors this function raises the error, instead of returning an error code.

io.lines ([filename, ⋯])

Opens the given file name in read mode and returns an iterator function that works like `file:lines(⋯)` over the opened file. When the iterator function detects the end of file, it returns no values (to finish the loop) and automatically closes the file.

The call `io.lines()` (with no file name) is equivalent to `io.input():lines("*l")`; that is, it iterates over the lines of the default input file. In this case it does not close the file when the loop ends.

In case of errors this function raises the error, instead of returning an error code.

io.open (filename [, mode])

This function opens a file, in the mode specified in the string `mode`. In case of success, it returns a new file handle.

The `mode` string can be any of the following:

> **"r"**: read mode (the default);
> **"w"**: write mode;
> **"a"**: append mode;
> **"r+"**: update mode, all previous data is preserved;
> **"w+"**: update mode, all previous data is erased;
> **"a+"**: append update mode, previous data is preserved, writing is only allowed at the end of file.

The `mode` string can also have a 'b' at the end, which is needed in some systems to open the file in binary mode.

io.output ([file])

Similar to `io.input`, but operates over the default output file.

io.popen (prog [, mode])

This function is system dependent and is not available on all platforms.

Starts program `prog` in a separated process and returns a file handle that you can use to read data from this program (if `mode` is "r", the default) or to write data to this program (if `mode` is "w").

io.read (⋯)

Equivalent to `io.input():read(⋯)`.

io.tmpfile ()

In case of success, returns a handle for a temporary file. This file is opened in update mode and it is automatically removed when the program ends.

io.type (obj)

Checks whether `obj` is a valid file handle. Returns the string `"file"` if `obj` is an open file handle, `"closed file"` if `obj` is a closed file handle, or **nil** if `obj` is not a file handle.

io.write (···)

Equivalent to `io.output():write(···)`.

file:close ()

Closes `file`. Note that files are automatically closed when their handles are garbage collected, but that takes an unpredictable amount of time to happen.

When closing a file handle created with `io.popen`, `file:close` returns the same values returned by `os.execute`.

file:flush ()

Saves any written data to `file`.

file:lines (···)

Returns an iterator function that, each time it is called, reads the file according to the given formats. When no format is given, uses "l" as a default. As an example, the construction

```
for c in file:lines(1) do body end
```

will iterate over all characters of the file, starting at the current position. Unlike `io.lines`, this function does not close the file when the loop ends.

In case of errors this function raises the error, instead of returning an error code.

file:read (···)

Reads the file `file`, according to the given formats, which specify what to read. For each format, the function returns a string or a number with the characters read, or **nil** if it cannot read data with the specified format. (In this latter case, the function does not read subsequent formats.) When called without formats, it uses a default format that reads the next line (see below).

The available formats are

> **"n":** reads a numeral and returns it as a float or an integer, following the lexical conventions of Lua. (The numeral may have leading spaces and a sign.) This format always reads the longest input sequence that is a valid prefix for a numeral; if that prefix does not form a valid numeral (e.g., an empty string, "0x", or "3.4e-"), it is discarded and the function returns **nil**.
> **"a":** reads the whole file, starting at the current position. On end of file, it returns the empty string.
> **"l":** reads the next line skipping the end of line, returning **nil** on end of file. This is the default format.
> **"L":** reads the next line keeping the end-of-line character (if present), returning **nil** on end of file.
> *number*: reads a string with up to this number of bytes, returning **nil** on end of file. If number is zero, it reads nothing and returns an empty string, or **nil** on end of file.

The formats "l" and "L" should be used only for text files.

file:seek ([whence [, offset]])

Sets and gets the file position, measured from the beginning of the file, to the position given by offset plus a base specified by the string whence, as follows:

"set": base is position 0 (beginning of the file);
"cur": base is current position;
"end": base is end of file;

In case of success, seek returns the final file position, measured in bytes from the beginning of the file. If seek fails, it returns **nil**, plus a string describing the error.

The default value for whence is "cur", and for offset is 0. Therefore, the call file:seek() returns the current file position, without changing it; the call file:seek("set") sets the position to the beginning of the file (and returns 0); and the call file:seek("end") sets the position to the end of the file, and returns its size.

file:setvbuf (mode [, size])

Sets the buffering mode for an output file. There are three available modes:

"no": no buffering; the result of any output operation appears immediately.
"full": full buffering; output operation is performed only when the buffer is full or when you explicitly flush the file (see io.flush).
"line": line buffering; output is buffered until a newline is output or there is any input from some special files (such as a terminal device).

For the last two cases, size specifies the size of the buffer, in bytes. The default is an appropriate size.

file:write (···)

Writes the value of each of its arguments to file. The arguments must be strings or numbers.

In case of success, this function returns file. Otherwise it returns **nil** plus a string describing the error.

6.9 – Operating System Facilities

This library is implemented through table os.

os.clock ()

Returns an approximation of the amount in seconds of CPU time used by the program.

os.date ([format [, time]])

Returns a string or a table containing date and time, formatted according to the given string format.

If the time argument is present, this is the time to be formatted (see the os.time function for a description of this value). Otherwise, date formats the current time.

If format starts with '!', then the date is formatted in Coordinated Universal Time. After this optional character, if format is the string "*t", then date returns a table with the following fields: year, month (1–12), day (1–31), hour (0–23), min (0–59), sec (0–61), wday (weekday, 1–7, Sunday is 1), yday (day of the year, 1–366), and isdst (daylight saving flag, a boolean). This last field may be absent if the information is not available.

If format is not "*t", then date returns the date as a string, formatted according to the same rules as the ISO C function strftime.

When called without arguments, date returns a reasonable date and time representation that depends on the host system and on the current locale. (More specifically, os.date() is equivalent to os.date("%c").)

On non-POSIX systems, this function may be not thread safe because of its reliance on C function gmtime and C function localtime.

os.difftime (t2, t1)

Returns the difference, in seconds, from time t1 to time t2 (where the times are values returned by os.time). In POSIX, Windows, and some other systems, this value is exactly t2-t1.

os.execute ([command])

This function is equivalent to the ISO C function system. It passes command to be executed by an operating system shell. Its first result is **true** if the command terminated successfully, or **nil** otherwise. After this first result the function returns a string plus a number, as follows:

> **"exit"**: the command terminated normally; the following number is the exit status of the command.
> **"signal"**: the command was terminated by a signal; the following number is the signal that terminated the command.

When called without a command, os.execute returns a boolean that is true if a shell is available.

os.exit ([code [, close]])

Calls the ISO C function exit to terminate the host program. If code is **true**, the returned status is EXIT_SUCCESS; if code is **false**, the returned status is EXIT_FAILURE; if code is a number, the returned status is this number. The default value for code is **true**.

If the optional second argument close is true, closes the Lua state before exiting.

os.getenv (varname)

Returns the value of the process environment variable varname, or **nil** if the variable is not defined.

os.remove (filename)

Deletes the file (or empty directory, on POSIX systems) with the given name. If this function fails, it returns **nil**, plus a string describing the error and the error code.

os.rename (oldname, newname)

Renames file or directory named oldname to newname. If this function fails, it returns **nil**, plus a string describing the error and the error code.

os.setlocale (locale [, category])

Sets the current locale of the program. locale is a system-dependent string specifying a locale; category is an optional string describing which category to change: "all", "collate", "ctype", "monetary", "numeric", or "time"; the default category is "all". The function returns the name of the new locale, or **nil** if the request cannot be honored.

If locale is the empty string, the current locale is set to an implementation-defined native locale. If locale is the string "C", the current locale is set to the standard C locale.

When called with **nil** as the first argument, this function only returns the name of the current locale for the given category.

This function may be not thread safe because of its reliance on C function `setlocale`.

os.time ([table])

Returns the current time when called without arguments, or a time representing the local date and time specified by the given table. This table must have fields `year`, `month`, and `day`, and may have fields `hour` (default is 12), `min` (default is 0), `sec` (default is 0), and `isdst` (default is **nil**). Other fields are ignored. For a description of these fields, see the `os.date` function.

The values in these fields do not need to be inside their valid ranges. For instance, if `sec` is -10, it means -10 seconds from the time specified by the other fields; if `hour` is 1000, it means +1000 hours from the time specified by the other fields.

The returned value is a number, whose meaning depends on your system. In POSIX, Windows, and some other systems, this number counts the number of seconds since some given start time (the "epoch"). In other systems, the meaning is not specified, and the number returned by `time` can be used only as an argument to `os.date` and `os.difftime`.

os.tmpname ()

Returns a string with a file name that can be used for a temporary file. The file must be explicitly opened before its use and explicitly removed when no longer needed.

On POSIX systems, this function also creates a file with that name, to avoid security risks. (Someone else might create the file with wrong permissions in the time between getting the name and creating the file.) You still have to open the file to use it and to remove it (even if you do not use it).

When possible, you may prefer to use `io.tmpfile`, which automatically removes the file when the program ends.

6.10 – The Debug Library

This library provides the functionality of the debug interface (§4.9) to Lua programs. You should exert care when using this library. Several of its functions violate basic assumptions about Lua code (e.g., that variables local to a function cannot be accessed from outside; that userdata metatables cannot be changed by Lua code; that Lua programs do not crash) and therefore can compromise otherwise secure code. Moreover, some functions in this library may be slow.

All functions in this library are provided inside the debug table. All functions that operate over a thread have an optional first argument which is the thread to operate over. The default is always the current thread.

debug.debug ()

Enters an interactive mode with the user, running each string that the user enters. Using simple commands and other debug facilities, the user can inspect global and local variables, change their values, evaluate expressions, and so on. A line containing only the word `cont` finishes this function, so that the caller continues its execution.

Note that commands for `debug.debug` are not lexically nested within any function and so have no direct access to local variables.

debug.gethook ([thread])

Returns the current hook settings of the thread, as three values: the current hook function, the current hook mask, and the current hook count (as set by the debug.sethook function).

debug.getinfo ([thread,] f [, what])

Returns a table with information about a function. You can give the function directly or you can give a number as the value of f, which means the function running at level f of the call stack of the given thread: level 0 is the current function (getinfo itself); level 1 is the function that called getinfo (except for tail calls, which do not count on the stack); and so on. If f is a number larger than the number of active functions, then getinfo returns **nil**.

The returned table can contain all the fields returned by lua_getinfo, with the string what describing which fields to fill in. The default for what is to get all information available, except the table of valid lines. If present, the option 'f' adds a field named func with the function itself. If present, the option 'L' adds a field named activelines with the table of valid lines.

For instance, the expression debug.getinfo(1,"n").name returns a name for the current function, if a reasonable name can be found, and the expression debug.getinfo(print) returns a table with all available information about the print function.

debug.getlocal ([thread,] f, local)

This function returns the name and the value of the local variable with index local of the function at level f of the stack. This function accesses not only explicit local variables, but also parameters, temporaries, etc.

The first parameter or local variable has index 1, and so on, following the order that they are declared in the code, counting only the variables that are active in the current scope of the function. Negative indices refer to vararg parameters; -1 is the first vararg parameter. The function returns **nil** if there is no variable with the given index, and raises an error when called with a level out of range. (You can call debug.getinfo to check whether the level is valid.)

Variable names starting with '(' (open parenthesis) represent variables with no known names (internal variables such as loop control variables, and variables from chunks saved without debug information).

The parameter f may also be a function. In that case, getlocal returns only the name of function parameters.

debug.getmetatable (value)

Returns the metatable of the given value or **nil** if it does not have a metatable.

debug.getregistry ()

Returns the registry table (see §4.5).

debug.getupvalue (f, up)

This function returns the name and the value of the upvalue with index up of the function f. The function returns **nil** if there is no upvalue with the given index.

Variable names starting with '(' (open parenthesis) represent variables with no known names (variables from chunks saved without debug information).

debug.getuservalue (u)

Returns the Lua value associated to u. If u is not a userdata, returns **nil**.

debug.sethook ([thread,] hook, mask [, count])

Sets the given function as a hook. The string `mask` and the number `count` describe when the hook will be called. The string mask may have any combination of the following characters, with the given meaning:

'c': the hook is called every time Lua calls a function;
'r': the hook is called every time Lua returns from a function;
'l': the hook is called every time Lua enters a new line of code.

Moreover, with a `count` different from zero, the hook is called also after every `count` instructions.

When called without arguments, `debug.sethook` turns off the hook.

When the hook is called, its first parameter is a string describing the event that has triggered its call: `"call"` (or `"tail call"`), `"return"`, `"line"`, and `"count"`. For line events, the hook also gets the new line number as its second parameter. Inside a hook, you can call `getinfo` with level 2 to get more information about the running function (level 0 is the `getinfo` function, and level 1 is the hook function).

debug.setlocal ([thread,] level, local, value)

This function assigns the value `value` to the local variable with index `local` of the function at level `level` of the stack. The function returns **nil** if there is no local variable with the given index, and raises an error when called with a `level` out of range. (You can call `getinfo` to check whether the level is valid.) Otherwise, it returns the name of the local variable.

See `debug.getlocal` for more information about variable indices and names.

debug.setmetatable (value, table)

Sets the metatable for the given `value` to the given `table` (which can be **nil**). Returns `value`.

debug.setupvalue (f, up, value)

This function assigns the value `value` to the upvalue with index `up` of the function `f`. The function returns **nil** if there is no upvalue with the given index. Otherwise, it returns the name of the upvalue.

debug.setuservalue (udata, value)

Sets the given `value` as the Lua value associated to the given `udata`. `udata` must be a full userdata.

Returns `udata`.

debug.traceback ([thread,] [message [, level]])

If `message` is present but is neither a string nor **nil**, this function returns `message` without further processing. Otherwise, it returns a string with a traceback of the call stack. The optional `message` string is appended at the beginning of the traceback. An optional `level` number tells at which level to start the traceback (default is 1, the function calling `traceback`).

debug.upvalueid (f, n)

Returns a unique identifier (as a light userdata) for the upvalue numbered n from the given function.

These unique identifiers allow a program to check whether different closures share upvalues. Lua closures that share an upvalue (that is, that access a same external local variable) will return identical ids for those upvalue indices.

debug.upvaluejoin (f1, n1, f2, n2)

Make the n1-th upvalue of the Lua closure f1 refer to the n2-th upvalue of the Lua closure f2.

7 – Lua Standalone

Although Lua has been designed as an extension language, to be embedded in a host C program, it is also frequently used as a standalone language. An interpreter for Lua as a standalone language, called simply lua, is provided with the standard distribution. The standalone interpreter includes all standard libraries, including the debug library. Its usage is:

```
lua [options] [script [args]]
```

The options are:

- -e *stat*: executes string *stat*;
- -l *mod*: "requires" *mod*;
- -i: enters interactive mode after running *script*;
- -v: prints version information;
- -E: ignores environment variables;
- --: stops handling options;
- -: executes stdin as a file and stops handling options.

After handling its options, lua runs the given *script*. When called without arguments, lua behaves as lua -v -i when the standard input (stdin) is a terminal, and as lua - otherwise.

When called without option -E, the interpreter checks for an environment variable LUA_INIT_5_3 (or LUA_INIT if the versioned name is not defined) before running any argument. If the variable content has the format @*filename*, then lua executes the file. Otherwise, lua executes the string itself.

When called with option -E, besides ignoring LUA_INIT, Lua also ignores the values of LUA_PATH and LUA_CPATH, setting the values of package.path and package.cpath with the default paths defined in luaconf.h.

All options are handled in order, except -i and -E. For instance, an invocation like

```
$ lua -e'a=1' -e 'print(a)' script.lua
```

will first set a to 1, then print the value of a, and finally run the file script.lua with no arguments. (Here $ is the shell prompt. Your prompt may be different.)

Before running any code, lua collects all command-line arguments in a global table called arg. The script name goes to index 0, the first argument after the script name goes to index 1, and so on. Any arguments before the script name (that is, the interpreter name plus its options) go to negative indices. For instance, in the call

```
$ lua -la b.lua t1 t2
```

the table is like this:

```
arg = { [-2] = "lua", [-1] = "-la",
        [0] = "b.lua",
        [1] = "t1", [2] = "t2" }
```

If there is no script in the call, the interpreter name goes to index 0, followed by the other arguments. For instance, the call

```
$ lua -e "print(arg[1])"
```

will print "-e". If there is a script, the script is called with parameters arg[1], ···, arg[#arg]. (Like all chunks in Lua, the script is compiled as a vararg function.)

In interactive mode, Lua repeatedly prompts and waits for a line. After reading a line, Lua first try to interpret the line as an expression. If it succeeds, it prints its value. Otherwise, it interprets the line as a statement. If you write an incomplete statement, the interpreter waits for its completion by issuing a different prompt.

If the global variable _PROMPT contains a string, then its value is used as the prompt. Similarly, if the global variable _PROMPT2 contains a string, its value is used as the secondary prompt (issued during incomplete statements).

In case of unprotected errors in the script, the interpreter reports the error to the standard error stream. If the error object is not a string but has a metamethod __tostring, the interpreter calls this metamethod to produce the final message. Otherwise, the interpreter converts the error object to a string and adds a stack traceback to it.

When finishing normally, the interpreter closes its main Lua state (see lua_close). The script can avoid this step by calling os.exit to terminate.

To allow the use of Lua as a script interpreter in Unix systems, the standalone interpreter skips the first line of a chunk if it starts with #. Therefore, Lua scripts can be made into executable programs by using chmod +x and the #! form, as in

```
#!/usr/local/bin/lua
```

(Of course, the location of the Lua interpreter may be different in your machine. If lua is in your PATH, then

```
#!/usr/bin/env lua
```

is a more portable solution.)

8 – Incompatibilities with the Previous Version

Here we list the incompatibilities that you may find when moving a program from Lua 5.2 to Lua 5.3. You can avoid some incompatibilities by compiling Lua with appropriate options (see file luaconf.h). However, all these compatibility options will be removed in the future.

Lua versions can always change the C API in ways that do not imply source-code changes in a program, such as the numeric values for constants or the implementation of functions as macros. Therefore, you should not assume that binaries are compatible between different Lua versions. Always recompile clients of the Lua API when using a new version.

Similarly, Lua versions can always change the internal representation of precompiled chunks; precompiled chunks are not compatible between different Lua versions.

The standard paths in the official distribution may change between versions.

8.1 – Changes in the Language

The main difference between Lua 5.2 and Lua 5.3 is the introduction of an integer subtype for numbers. Although this change should not affect "normal" computations, some computations (mainly those that involve some kind of overflow) can give different results.

You can fix these differences by forcing a number to be a float (in Lua 5.2 all numbers were float), in particular writing constants with an ending .0 or using x = x + 0.0 to convert a variable. (This recommendation is only for a quick fix for an occasional incompatibility; it is not a general guideline for good programming. For good programming, use floats where you need floats and integers where you need integers.)

The conversion of a float to a string now adds a .0 suffix to the result if it looks like an integer. (For instance, the float 2.0 will be printed as 2.0, not as 2.) You should always use an explicit format when you need a specific format for numbers.

(Formally this is not an incompatibility, because Lua does not specify how numbers are formatted as strings, but some programs assumed a specific format.)

The generational mode for the garbage collector was removed. (It was an experimental feature in Lua 5.2.)

8.2 – Changes in the Libraries

The bit32 library has been deprecated. It is easy to require a compatible external library or, better yet, to replace its functions with appropriate bitwise operations. (Keep in mind that bit32 operates on 32-bit integers, while the bitwise operators in Lua 5.3 operate on Lua integers, which by default have 64 bits.)

The Table library now respects metamethods for setting and getting elements.

The ipairs iterator now respects metamethods and its __ipairs metamethod has been deprecated.

Option names in io.read do not have a starting '*' anymore. For compatibility, Lua will continue to accept (and ignore) this character.

The following functions were deprecated in the mathematical library: atan2, cosh, sinh, tanh, pow, frexp, and ldexp. You can replace math.pow(x,y) with x^y; you can replace math.atan2 with math.atan, which now accepts one or two parameters; you can replace `math.ldexp(x,exp)` with `x * 2.0^exp`. For the other operations, you can either use an external library or implement them in Lua.

The searcher for C loaders used by `require` changed the way it handles versioned names. Now, the version should come after the module name (as is usual in most other tools). For compatibility, that searcher still tries the old format if it cannot find an open function according to the new style. (Lua 5.2 already worked that way, but it did not document the change.)

The call `collectgarbage("count")` now returns only one result. (You can compute that second result from the fractional part of the first result.)

8.3 – Changes in the API

Continuation functions now receive as parameters what they needed to get through `lua_getctx`, so `lua_getctx` has been removed. Adapt your code accordingly.

Function `lua_dump` has an extra parameter, `strip`. Use 0 as the value of this parameter to get the old behavior.

Functions to inject/project unsigned integers (`lua_pushunsigned`, `lua_tounsigned`, `lua_tounsignedx`, `luaL_checkunsigned`, `luaL_optunsigned`) were deprecated. Use their signed equivalents with a type cast.

Macros to project non-default integer types (`luaL_checkint`, `luaL_optint`, `luaL_checklong`, `luaL_optlong`) were deprecated. Use their equivalent over `lua_Integer` with a type cast (or, when possible, use `lua_Integer` in your code).

9 – The Complete Syntax of Lua

Here is the complete syntax of Lua in extended BNF. As usual in extended BNF, {A} means 0 or more As, and [A] means an optional A. (For operator precedences, see §3.4.8; for a description of the terminals Name, Numeral, and LiteralString, see §3.1.)

```
chunk ::= block

block ::= {stat} [retstat]

stat ::=  ‘;’ |
          varlist ‘=’ explist |
          functioncall |
          label |
          break |
          goto Name |
          do block end |
          while exp do block end |
          repeat block until exp |
          if exp then block {elseif exp then block} [else block] end |
          for Name ‘=’ exp ‘,’ exp [‘,’ exp] do block end |
          for namelist in explist do block end |
          function funcname funcbody |
          local function Name funcbody |
          local namelist [‘=’ explist]

retstat ::= return [explist] [‘;’]

label ::= ‘::’ Name ‘::’

funcname ::= Name {‘.’ Name} [‘:’ Name]

varlist ::= var {‘,’ var}

var ::=  Name | prefixexp ‘[’ exp ‘]’ | prefixexp ‘.’ Name

namelist ::= Name {‘,’ Name}

explist ::= exp {‘,’ exp}

exp ::=  nil | false | true | Numeral | LiteralString | ‘...’ | functiondef |
         prefixexp | tableconstructor | exp binop exp | unop exp

prefixexp ::= var | functioncall | ‘(’ exp ‘)’

functioncall ::=  prefixexp args | prefixexp ‘:’ Name args

args ::=  ‘(’ [explist] ‘)’ | tableconstructor | LiteralString

functiondef ::= function funcbody

funcbody ::= ‘(’ [parlist] ‘)’ block end
```

```
parlist ::= namelist [',' '...'] | '...'

tableconstructor ::= '{' [fieldlist] '}'

fieldlist ::= field {fieldsep field} [fieldsep]

field ::= '[' exp ']' '=' exp | Name '=' exp | exp

fieldsep ::= ',' | ';'

binop ::=  '+' | '-' | '*' | '/' | '//' | '^' | '%' |
           '&' | '~' | '|' | '>>' | '<<' | '..' |
           '<' | '<=' | '>' | '>=' | '==' | '~=' |
           and | or

unop ::= '-' | not | '#' | '~'
```

www.ingramcontent.com/pod-product-compliance
Lightning Source LLC
Chambersburg PA
CBHW060201060326
40690CB00018B/4194